THE
SILVER
LINING

THE SILVER LINING

An
Innovation
Playbook
for
Uncertain
Times

SCOTT D. ANTHONY

HARVARD BUSINESS PRESS
BOSTON, MASSACHUSETTS

13 12 11 10 09   5 4 3 2

Library of Congress Cataloging-in-Publication Data
Anthony, Scott D.
  The silver lining : an innovation playbook for uncertain times / Scott
  D. Anthony.
     p. cm.
  ISBN 978-1-4221-3901-1 (hardcover : alk. paper)
1. Technological innovations—Management—Case studies.
2. Disruptive technologies—Management—Case studies. 3. New
products—Case studies. 4. Business planning. I. Title.
  HD45.A68 2009
  658.4'063—dc22   2009000466

CONTENTS

INTRODUCTION

I wasn't supposed to write this book.

I was supposed to be in the midst of my first semester as a doctoral student at the Harvard Business School, filling whatever idle hours I had with activities at Innosight. I had planned for the transition for almost two years and was confident in my decision. Until one weekend in July, when it became clear to me that continuing in my role at Innosight presented the best platform to help managers improve their ability to successfully innovate.

In the midst of the market meltdown in October, my mother asked me if I still thought I had made the right choice.

"How do you feel about walking away from a recession-proof industry?" she asked.

"I haven't even thought about it," I replied.

I wasn't focused on what could have been; I was focused on helping innovators figure out what the economic crisis meant to them. The media was filled with a steady drumbeat of negative news, but even a cursory glance at previous downturns suggested that there were clear rays of hope. Of course, realizing that hope required thinking and acting differently. Thus, the idea for a book providing practical assistance for innovation in uncertain times.

In Gratitude

The tools in this book all trace back to fieldwork with top-flight innovation practitioners. I am particularly grateful to my friends at Procter & Gamble, especially George Glackin, Terry Lynch, Mark Dawes, Karl Ronn, Bruce Brown, Beth Combs, Jessica Sams, John Leikhim, Greg Icenhower, Charlotte Otto, Mike Grieff, Joanna Zucker, Gil Cloyd, Marie Harris, Gary Coombe, Melanie Healey, Judy Miller, Marc Pritchard, Mike DiPaola, Sue Ede, Tom Dierking, Nancy McCarthy, Dave Caracci, Alan Goldstein, Anne Lilly Cone, Stephanie Connaughton, Karen Gallagher, David Dintenfass, Jill Boughton, Daisuke Otobe, and Dave Nichols. I hope I have taught them a fraction of what they have taught me. Special thanks also go to longtime friends Michael Putz from Cisco Systems (whose research into leadership development forms the backbone of chapter 8), Tyler England from Hewlett-Packard, Eleanor Cippel and Mark Contreras from Scripps, Dave Goulait, Clark Gilbert, Dick Foster, and Steve Kraus.

My colleagues at Innosight are a consistent source of inspiration. I owe particular thanks to Natalie Painchaud, who uncovered great historical stories; Tim Huse, who helped with key analyses; Steve Wunker, who made invaluable comments on the manuscript; Joe Sinfield, who provided key insights into the concepts in chapter 3; and Matt Eyring, who developed the conceptual underpinning of chapter 7. Of course, all of us at Innosight remain perpetually thankful that Clayton Christensen and Mark Johnson conspired to send us on this journey almost a decade ago.

Jacque Murphy and Kathleen Carr from Harvard Business Press have been critical thought partners throughout the book's development. They deserve praise for moving so quickly to make this book a reality. Stephani Finks came up with the creative idea for the shimmering cover, and Allison Peter helped to polish *The Silver Lining*.

I finished the second draft of the manuscript in late December at my parents' home in Maryland, surrounded by four siblings and their partners, seven nieces and nephews, my parents, three dogs, and five puppies. It was as wonderfully chaotic as it sounds. Mom, Dad, Tricia, John, Michelle, Scott, Mike, Jess, Pete, David, thanks as always.

To my children, Charlie and Holly: There's simply nothing more gratifying than seeing smiles break out on your faces when I return home from a long day at work. You make your father happier than you'll ever know.

Finally, to my wife Joanne: It is hard for me to believe it has been ten years since I coaxed you to move from your home in England to what has become our home in Boston. There isn't a day that goes by when I don't say a silent prayer for whatever it was that allowed life to unfold in a way that we ended up together. When my own dark clouds roll in, you are my silver lining. I continually strive to be as good a husband and father as you are a wife and mother.

To Joanne.

The Great Disruption

National Cash Register was formed in the midst of the "Semi-Panic" of 1884. Apple launched its iPod in 2001. Tough times don't stop innovation. Managing in the Great Disruption requires companies to master constant change—or suffer the consequences.

My three-year-old son usually begins the day with boundless optimism. He bounces out of bed, gets his breakfast, and is ready to take on the world. As it brightens outside (yes, he's usually up before 6 a.m.), he inevitably goes to the window. If it is a gloomy day, he will turn around with a forlorn look on his face and say, "Daddy, the dark clouds have rolled in" (a phrase taught to him by Ms. Wendy at day care).

For companies passionate about growth and innovation, the dark clouds indeed rolled in last year. As financial titans fell, Wall Street trembled, Main Street froze, consumers and investors panicked, and everyone seemed to hesitate while waiting for stability to return, the notion that innovation must be entering a period of dormancy seemed inevitable.

Historians appropriately termed the economic wasteland of the 1930s the Great Depression. Output shrunk, unemployment rose, and people fought hard just to get a job. It wasn't a completely chaotic time, however. If you compare the list of companies that made up the Dow Jones Industrial Average in July 1930 to the July 1939 list, you would see that twenty-two of the thirty companies remained the same.

While the 2000s prior to 2008 have had economic and geopolitical shocks, just about everyone would agree that the economic situation was substantially more stable than that during the Great Depression. Yet, if you compared the companies that constituted the Dow Jones Industrial Average in July 1999 to the July 2008 list, you would see that twenty-two of the thirty companies remained the same.[1]

In other words, the past decade's stability was a mirage; there wasn't really much calm before the storm. Over the past decade, technological improvements and a stark increase in venture capital financing have made starting and scaling businesses easier than ever. The rise of Brazil, Russia, China, India, and other emerging markets mean market leaders have to deal with more sharp-elbowed competitors than ever before. Industries are frantically converging and colliding. These changes have made it harder for great companies to maintain greatness. Leaders in a range of industries can attest that they have been grappling with the effect of these forces for some time.

Consider Microsoft (which became a component of the Dow Jones average in November 1999). A decade ago, the only threat to the company seemed to be the prospect of a breakup orchestrated by the U.S. Justice Department. The company has grown steadily over the past decade, from $15 billion in revenues in 1998 to $60 billion in revenues in its most recently completed fiscal year. It has built big businesses in new markets like mobile phones, video gaming, and home entertainment. Its reward? A stock price that has decreased relative to the market among widespread concern that there is no way the company can counter the threat posed by Google.

Or think about beleaguered newspaper companies. The emergence of the Internet in the late 1990s seemed to be an obvious threat to most companies. Yet by 2002, most newspaper companies had launched successful Web sites and enjoyed operating margins approaching 30 percent. Today the industry is fighting for its very survival. Tribune Company, whose diversified media properties include the *Los Angeles Times,* the *Chicago Tribune,* and WGN America, went bankrupt in late 2008. In 2005, Lee Enterprises purchased Pulitzer Inc.—a company two-thirds its size—for roughly $1.5 billion. By the end of 2008, the combined entity was worth about $75 million.

An appropriate name for today's times is the Great Disruption. Change is ripping through markets at unprecedented pace. Competitive advantage that took decades to build disappears seemingly overnight. While output might shrink and unemployment is sure to rise, companies that master these forces still have a chance to thrive; those that don't are sure to struggle.

No one is certain yet how the malady facing the global economy will play out. The worst might be behind us; it might not. Regardless, many companies are going to face severe challenges. Does that mean that would-be innovators should go into deep hibernation? Instead of thinking of the next great thing, should innovators hide out in seemingly safe operating roles until the current storm passes? Not if history is any guide.

Historical Signs of Hope

Innovation can flourish, even in the toughest of economic climates. This section highlights new companies or innovations launched in past downturns and shows how the last few downturns didn't hold back "on the brink" attackers that were transforming current markets or creating new ones.

Businesses Forming, Innovations Launching

Step back to the early 1880s. The past decade had been chaotic. The Great Panic of 1873 resulted in a sixty-five-month downturn. The early 1880s featured economic expansion, but the country slipped back into recession in 1884. The 1883–1884 recession wasn't quite as severe as the contraction of the 1870s, but it was severe enough that some historians called 1884 the "Semi-Panic." A *New York Times* article in 1911 looking at past economic downturns noted, "The great activity existing from 1878 to 1882 began to cease in 1883, and by the early part of 1884 there was a curtailment in almost every branch of trade. Failures began to increase, several railroads went into receiverships, while the most striking feature of all was the drop in the price of securities, and especially of commodities. For example, the price of steel rails dropped from $71 in 1880 to $35 at the close of 1888."[2]

It would seem like a terrible time to introduce an expensive new product into the market. But brothers John and Frank Patterson sensed an opportunity. The country's transition from an agrarian economy was driving substantial growth in the retail industry. The Patterson brothers' experience running a general store in one of their coal yards exposed them to a long-term problem facing retailers across the country: managing cash. At the time, retailers' registers were nothing more than wooden drawers that held bills and coins. Employees could easily take a couple of bills from the till without the retail owner ever knowing about it. In fact, it was hard for store owners to really know with any degree of certainty whether they were operating at a profit or a loss.

Here's how John Patterson described the problem: "At the end of three years, although we had sold annually about $50,000 worth of goods on which there was a large margin, we found ourselves worse off than nothing. . . One day I found several bread tickets lying around loose, and discovered that our oldest clerk was favoring his friends by selling below the regular prices. Another day I noticed a certain credit customer buying groceries. At night, on looking over the blotter, I found that the clerk had forgotten to make any entry of it. This set me to thinking that the goods might often go out of the store in this way—without our ever getting a cent for them."[3]

Some retailers developed complex systems to help minimize theft. For example, large retailers would physically separate clerks who dealt with customers from cordoned-off cashiers who handled money. They would employ "cash children" who would hand-deliver money to the cashier and bring the clerk change, a sales voucher, and the wrapped goods (the cashiers were often colocated with wrapping desks). More advanced retailers would use what was known as the "Lamson cash-basket system," which involved wire-pulley systems that brought money in steel cages to store owners or trusted employees.[4]

In 1878, James Ritty, a Dayton tavern keeper, was on an ocean liner bound for Europe.[5] Ritty noticed a device that made a notation every time the ship's propeller rotated. Intrigued by the concept, Ritty and his brother invented a mechanical device patented in 1879 as "Ritty's Incorruptible Cashier." Ritty's original device was fairly rudimental, with no cash drawer. Further versions added a cash drawer and paper rolls to record transactions, which would make theft more difficult and provide retailers much greater control over their operations. Ritty sold his business in 1882 to a local china and glassware salesman.

The Patterson brothers were early customers of Ritty's machines. The register sold for $100, which in today's terms is about $2,500. As John Patterson noted, "One day we received a circular from someone in Dayton, Ohio, advertising a machine which recorded money and sales in retail stores. The price was $100. We telegraphed for two of them, and when we saw them we were astonished at the cost. They were made mostly of wood, had no cash drawer, and were very crude. But we put them in the store, and, in spite of their deficiencies, at the end of twelve months we cleared $6,000."[6] As their coal and railroad investments declined in 1884, the Patterson brothers decided to purchase Ritty's company for about $6,500, rename it National Cash Register, and commercialize the mechanical cash register. NCR went on to dominate this new market, which helped to accelerate the modernization of the retailing industry. By 1911, it had sold more than 1 million machines and had 95 percent of the market. Thomas J. Watson Sr., who would go on to transform IBM into a technology powerhouse during his thirty-year reign as president, developed his legendary sales skills at NCR. Today, NCR has more than $6 billion in annual revenue.

The story is timeless. A deep-seated customer problem coupled with a novel way to address that problem. Customer problems don't fade in tough economic times; in fact, tough economic times can highlight previously hidden problems or cause old problems to intensify. Petty theft that is a nagging problem in booming times becomes a make-or-break issue as money gets tighter. Companies might think that customers flee to safety and become uninterested in innovative ideas when times get tough. However, longitudinal research by market research company Nielsen suggests that is not the case. The research shows that U.K. and U.S. consumers stated intention to purchase innovative products, and the value they perceive in new products has remained remarkably stable over the past thirty years.[7]

NCR isn't an isolated example. Twenty-five of the companies that made up the Dow Jones Industrial Average in December 2008 were formed since the National Bureau of Economic Research (NBER) started tracking economic cycles in the United States. Thirteen of those twenty-five, including 3M, General Electric, Microsoft, and Walt Disney, were formed in a year that featured an economic downturn.[8]

Many other notable companies came into being in economically difficult years. A partial list of companies formed in the United States in a year featuring a recession includes Ann Taylor, Bain & Company, Black & Decker, Bridgestone Tire, Church & Dwight, Colgate-Palmolive, Compaq, ConAgra Foods, Cummins, Digital Equipment Corporation, Dow Chemical, Dow Jones, Electronic Arts, Eli Lilly, Enterprise Rent-A-Car, Harley-Davidson, iRobot, Johnson Controls, Marvel Entertainment, Mattel, McKinsey & Co., Merrill Lynch, Newell Rubbermaid, Post Cereals, Progressive, RCA, Scott Paper, Starwood Hotels & Resorts Worldwide, Texas Instruments, The Hershey Company, Toys "R" Us, and Whole Foods Market.

Further, a number of game-changing product, service, or business model innovations were developed or launched in tough economic climates. In 1876, Alexander Graham Bell developed the technology underpinning the modern telephone. Eastman Kodak launched its Brownie camera, which transformed the world of photography, in 1900. McDonald's pioneered its fast-food service technique under the name "Speedee Service System" in 1948 (discussed in more depth in chapter 7). Sony introduced its transistor radio in 1957.

Procter & Gamble introduced Pampers brand disposable diapers in 1961. IBM launched its first personal computer in 1981. Nokia introduced its first car phone in 1982. Apple launched the first version of the iPod in 2001.

On-the-Brink Disruptors Surging

Many of the developments detailed fit the pattern of "disruptive innovation" (see "Disruption Defined" for an overview). Disruptive innovators bring something completely different to a market. Instead of trying to play the innovation game *better* than existing competitors, the disruptor *changes the game*. Disruptors typically transform existing markets or create new ones by focusing on convenience, simplicity, accessibility, or affordability. Academic research and Innosight fieldwork show that disruptive innovation is the more reliable way to create new growth businesses.[9]

It's natural to assume that tough times would be particularly hard on up-and-coming disruptive companies that have had some early success but haven't broken through to the mainstream. After all, consumers and companies snapping collective wallets shut would surely take the wind out of the sails of still unfamiliar up-and-comers.

History suggests otherwise. Innosight analyzed how up-and-coming disruptors (defined as disruptive companies with revenues of less than $1 billion) did in the face of the last three economic downturns in the United States (as dated by the NBER to cover 1980–1982, 1990, and 2001).[10]

In 1979, eleven such companies, such as Intel, Home Depot, Nucor, and Southwest Airlines, fit the criteria. Revenues of

DISRUPTION DEFINED

Harvard Business School professor Clayton Christensen identified the pattern of disruptive innovation through research in the hard-disk industry. In that research, summarized in the 1997 book *The Innovator's Dilemma,* Christensen determined that market leaders almost always won when the battle involved bringing a product that offered improvement along traditional performance dimensions to leading customers.[11] Christensen termed these improvements *sustaining* innovations, because they sustained an incumbent's business model. Christensen found that market leaders almost always lost when the battle involved bringing a product that was worse along traditional performance dimensions (e.g., disk capacity), but better along different performance dimensions (e.g., size). These innovations tended to take root in different markets that uniquely valued the new performance dimensions. Christensen called these *disruptive* innovations because they disrupted and redefined what constituted quality.

Subsequent research and fieldwork have identified more than two hundred disruptive developments over the past fifty years across a range of industries. Some disruptions, like discount retailing (Wal-Mart), low-cost automobiles (Toyota), steel mini-mills (Nucor), and digital music (Apple), reshape existing markets. Other disruptions, like personal computers, online advertising (Google), and online auctions (eBay), create entirely new markets.

the eleven companies grew at a compound annual rate of 22 percent between 1979 and 1982. Between 1989 and 1991, the sample of eleven up-and-coming disruptors, which included Best Buy, Cisco, and Charles Schwab, grew revenues by 33 percent. Investors who spotted these companies earned hefty returns. Investing $10,000 in the nine companies in the sample that were publicly traded at the end of 1989 and another $10,000 in Cisco when it went public in early 1990, would turn $100,000 into almost $300,000 by the end of 1991 (a tidy 72 percent annual return). A similar investment in the S&P 500 would have turned $100,000 into about $120,000.

The pattern continued in the 2001 downturn. Between 2000 and 2002, twenty-three up-and-coming disruptors such as Google, Amazon.com, and Research In Motion (the manufacturer of the popular BlackBerry line of products) grew revenues by 32 percent.

Our sample is heavily biased, but still the directional results are interesting.[12] If you are an investor or analyst, it suggests paying careful attention to up-and-coming disruptors that have built a solid base from which to drive further growth, such as Alibaba.com, iRobot, EnerNOC, K[12] Inc., First Solar, Facebook, and LinkedIn (some of these companies are highlighted in more depth in chapter 9). If you work for an operating company that is debating whether to postpone disruptive innovation efforts until better times arrive, be careful. You might be missing powerful growth opportunities and creating space for competitors to create substantial competitive advantages in tomorrow's great growth markets.

Scarcity and the Silver Lining

The gloom that pervades the Anthony household when the dark clouds roll in doesn't last long. Maybe we won't go to the park, but we'll have a chance to do puzzles, read books, or watch Daddy make a fool of himself playing Guitar Hero on the Wii.

Common wisdom suggests that every crisis presents opportunities. Consider the effects of a raging forest fire as an analogy. Sure, there is destruction, but the soil left behind is fertile, helping to create the next generation of giants. Fires can remove deadwood and tangled brush that constrained growth. Plants requiring direct sunlight can prosper. For these reasons, the U.S. Department of Agriculture often allows lightning fires to burn in monitored areas.

Perhaps the good times are in fact dead. And certainly someone thinking of forming the umpteenth "Web 2.0-widget-to-grab-audience-and-find-advertisers" ought to pause and think about whether they really have a defined competitive advantage that can translate into a sustainable business.

But real customers continue to face real problems. And as always, innovators who figure out different ways to solve those problems—and make money doing so—will have opportunities to create new growth businesses.

Cisco Systems CEO John Chambers believes that downturns present substantial opportunities for forward-thinking companies. In a November 2008 interview, Chambers described how Cisco historically has become more aggressive in investments in business opportunities during downturns.

"Remember the Asian financial crisis in 1997?" Chambers said. "Most of the economies in the area were contracting. I knew that Cisco's peers were making a potentially major mistake by dramatically cutting back their resources there, so we did the reverse. Straight into the economic downturn, we decided to increase our resources and send a number of senior executives to expand our presence in the region. Within a year, we gained the number-one market position in almost all of the Asian countries, and we never gave it up."[13]

The challenge does seem stark. Corporations have to figure out how to do more with less. They have to continue to invest in the future while ensuring that they have a right to *have* a future. Entrepreneurs have to create new growth businesses without ample capital.

The biggest silver lining for innovation is that the scarcity that is sure to result from the current economic climate is actually a *good thing* for innovation. Abundance is actually the *root cause* of many corporate struggles with innovation. Too much time or money allows companies to continue to follow fatally flawed strategies for too long or create overly complicated solutions that actually overshoot customer needs.

On the other hand, constraints are one of the great enablers of innovation. As an example, think about the retailing industry. Over the past one hundred years, the industry has been a source of significant business model innovations, such as Wal-Mart's discount model, Costco's warehouse club model, Inditex's Zara fast fashion model, and Amazon.com's collect-cash-before-you-contact-suppliers model.

Why is the retailing industry such fertile ground for business model innovation? At least one explanation is scarcity. The basic retailing model makes it very difficult for retailers to innovate the features and functionalities of the products they sell. A constrained environment has funneled creativity to where it can best be applied, creating powerful waves of growth.

Similarly, why are entrepreneurs so good at rapidly iterating their strategies? Is it because they are just more flexible than people inside established companies? No. Entrepreneurs have no choice. If they don't rapidly change course, they will run out of money. The discipline that bad times force can allow companies to impose sharper constraints that inspire creativity.

Amazon.com founder Jeff Bezos has experienced the dizzying highs of the dot.com bubble and the lows that followed the bubble bursting. He believes that constraints can help to spur innovation. "A lot of invention doesn't have to be expensive. That's just one of the constraints you have to invent inside of," Bezos says. "If you ever find yourself in a box, the best way to get out of the box is to invent your way out of the box. Either/or thinking is very constraining. Sometimes people say it is either A or B and you instead have to invent C."[14]

While venture capital funding might slow, again perhaps that's not a bad thing. As venture capitalists have grown over the past decade, many have gotten away from their roots of providing seed capital to small start-up companies. Instead, they fight fiercely to fund proved later-stage companies that really don't need the capital or rush to provide me-too funding to companies jumping into already crowded markets.

Flooding a flawed idea with venture capital doesn't make it a good idea. And companies that invest hundreds of millions of dollars into a strategy find it harder to correct course once they inevitably find out that the strategy that looked perfect on paper doesn't look so good in the market. Research by consulting company Booz Allen Hamilton shows almost no relation between a company's investment in research and development and its performance.[15]

There's never been a better time for innovators to face tighter purse strings. The world of innovation has changed substantially since the last global recession in 2001. Innovation can happen much more quickly and cheaply. Tools like prediction markets, collaboration software, design tools, virtual focus groups, and markets of low-cost specialists can dramatically expedite the innovation process. Facebook was able to go from a business in a dorm room to a community with millions of members in less than five years. In early 2007, entrepreneurial guru Guy Kawasaki launched a business spending $15,000. In late 2008, teen "blogger/ entrepreneur" Jessica Mah spent a whopping $500 to launch an internship job board. Kawasaki's business wasn't a big success and Mah's business (at the time of the writing of this book) is very much a work in progress, but that's not the point. The point is that entrepreneurs and corporate innovators have never had more affordable ways to take an idea forward.

One message that will repeat throughout this book is that guidance about innovating in uncertain times is actually guidance for innovating in *any* economic climate. Tough economic times are going to force innovators to do what they should have been doing already.

The Transformation Imperative

The challenge is steep. In the 1980s and 1990s, companies could grow bottom-line profits by focusing on operational excellence. Today, most well-run companies have very little fat left to cut. In the Great Disruption, that leaves companies with a choice: live with shrinking profits and increasing chances of extinction or follow a different approach.

For many companies, the challenge is steeper than simply eking out incremental improvements or expanding into new markets. The challenge is reinvention, or transformation. Simply doing what companies are doing better won't be enough. Companies have to fundamentally do something quite different from today. Perpetual transformation is the only way to thrive during the Great Disruption. Even in healthy economic times, standing still was becoming less of an option as competition intensified and industries collided.

Unfortunately, the brutal reality is that most efforts at transformation fail miserably. Just about every manager has lived through a transformation effort that starts brimming with unbridled hope and ends in crashing disappointment.

A survey Innosight administered in late 2008 with *Forbes* illustrates the basic challenge.[16] The survey found that close to 80 percent of respondents recognized the fundamental need for transformation. About two-thirds of respondents reported allocating resources toward transformation. But only 12 percent of respondents reported making excellent progress in their transformation efforts. Further, 80 percent of respondents reported that the current economic climate was increasing the *need* for transformation, even if toughening times held the amount of *resources* for transformation constant.

There are signs of hope. The company most widely cited in the Innosight survey as successfully transforming itself was Apple. Indeed, the period from 2003 to 2008 was absolutely remarkable for a company that limped along during most of the 1990s. Its market capitalization increased from roughly $5 billion to roughly $150 billion. While a nontrivial portion of that growth came because Apple dramatically improved the performance of its core computing operations, the lion's share of credit goes to the creation of new growth businesses. Apple launched its first iPod player in 2001, it opened the virtual door of its iTunes online music store in 2003, and it launched its iPhone smartphone in 2007. Each of those launches became a platform for successive generations of innovations that drove Apple's phenomenal growth.

IBM is another company often cited as having mastered perpetual transformation. The company frequently enters into new businesses and categories. Its latest widespread transformation traces back to challenging times in the late 1980s and early 1990s. The company faced intensifying competition in many of its core categories. While the old saying, "No one gets fired for hiring IBM" still held, many other competitors had reached the level of quality where they too were viable purchase options. IBM responded by accelerating its move into service businesses. Today, close to 60 percent of its revenue comes from services (aided by a 2002 purchase of PricewaterhouseCoopers). It also formed a group called Emerging Business Opportunities to enter into new markets. That group has helped IBM create substantial businesses around open-source software, wireless, life sciences, and grid computing.

Notice a connection? Transformation comes from entering new markets and leaving old ones. Companies rarely transform themselves through cost cutting or improved operational effectiveness. Operational effectiveness is necessary to compete, and world-class operators can create competitive advantage, but in almost all cases, operational effectiveness is insufficient to stave off disruption and drive long-term competitive advantage.[17]

The pattern continues. Another company flagged in the Innosight survey was Procter & Gamble. Founded more than 170 years ago, the consumer packaged-goods titan is constantly launching new brands and evaluating which businesses it should exit. During the 2000s, it sold off consumer staples such as food shortening (Crisco), peanut butter (Jif), and coffee (Folgers), and accelerated investments in higher-margin health and beauty products. It acquired Wella and its professional hair-care products in 2003 and Gillette men's grooming brands in 2005.

As of this writing, Pampers was P&G's biggest brand. P&G's biggest competitor in the diaper business is Kimberly-Clark (KC), which produces Huggies, Kleenex tissues, and Scott paper towels. If you go back to the 1980s, it wasn't obvious that KC was destined to be a critical P&G competitor. At the time, most of KC's business involved making commodity paper that served as an input for other consumer products companies. KC expanded its efforts into branded consumer products and grew substantially.

One of KC's competitors in the paper business in the early 1980s was a Finnish conglomerate that primarily focused on making products derived from natural products, such as rubber boots. In one of the most unlikely transformations in business history, the company entered into the mobile phone market. That company—Nokia—is today one of the world's leading technology companies.

While Nokia and KC successfully transformed themselves and reaped the rewards, a third paper company focused on operational effectiveness. International Paper has profit margins and other operating statistics that rival any paper player. But while Nokia and KC created billions of dollars of value, International Paper largely languished.

These examples are not meant to suggest that transformation is easy. It is not. More often than not companies fail when they try to go beyond their core business.[18] But in the Great Disruption, companies don't really have a choice. Investing in transformational efforts in a brutal market appears difficult, but the alternative isn't stagnation, it is extinction.

An Innovation Playbook for Uncertain Times

The Great Disruption creates real challenges for managers who have made a career out of focused execution. Smart management and prudent cost controls might have been enough to survive the Great Depression, but they are wholly insufficient for surviving the Great Disruption. For example, all the operational acumen in the world hasn't helped U.S. newspaper companies handle the seismic shifts in their industry.

A good way to visualize what is required is to think about what a classically trained musician needs to do to become an effective jazz musician. The musician has the right foundational knowledge and practical ability to make the transition. Continuing to play with accuracy and following principles of good musicianship continue to be important. But the transformation-seeking musician has to *stop* certain behaviors, such as following carefully laid-out scripts displayed in music scores. The musician has to *change* the way he uses his ears. Instead of listening to ensure that everyone is playing in synch with each other, a jazz musician listens for unexpected changes. Finally, the musician has to *start* a new behavior—improvisation based on his personal synthesis of a variety of music styles. The transformation is possible. Jazz greats such as Wynton Marsalis, Herbie Hancock, Scott Joplin, and Shirley Horn were classically trained musicians. But it requires careful thinking and hard work.

Similarly, for leaders to move from the business equivalent of classical music (operational effectiveness) to jazz (innovation), there are things they need to stop, do differently, and start. Specifically, companies have to stop some innovation efforts to free up time and money for transformation (chapter 2). They have to do more with less by improving the productivity of individual innovation initiatives and broader innovation programs (chapters 3 through 6). They have to start "loving the low end" to reach value-seeking customer segments (chapter 7). Individuals need to start driving personal reinvention so they have the fluidity to master increasingly common paradoxes (chapter 8).

While mastering innovation has never been easy, today's leaders have it tougher than ever. A rocky economic climate constrains budgets. Intense competition leaves little margin for error. Impatient stockholders lessen the risk tolerance of almost any sane executive. In the face of these challenges, growth-seeking executives face the seemingly impossible task of paring costs to the bone, while simultaneously planting and nurturing seeds of tomorrow's growth businesses. It's no surprise that most companies struggle to master these seemingly discordant challenges.

This book is intended to be a guide for executives and innovators seeking to seize the silver lining in today's difficult times, for strategists and investors trying to spot industry winners and losers, and for individuals thinking about how to tighten their own belts or reinvent themselves.

Wishing times were better is not particularly helpful. Pretending times haven't changed won't do innovators any good either. There's no doubt that some potentially game-changing companies will fail before cracking into the mainstream, or that an entrepreneur with a great idea will struggle to find financing. But those that manage the Great Disruption in the right way still have substantial opportunities. It is going to get tougher, and the bar for success is going to get higher. But there remain ample opportunities to be seized by those who don't freeze.

2

Prune Prudently

Which would you shut down? A project with first-year revenues of $220,000 or one with first-year revenues of $200 million? What if you knew the smaller project (Google) would change the world and the larger project (Vanilla Coke) would eventually be discontinued? Downturns require prudent pruning of portfolios to free up scarce resources.

When times get tough, one of the first things each of us think about is what we can do without. Maybe I don't need to pay for three hundred cable channels. Perhaps I could cut latte consumption from five a week to two. Similarly, the Great Disruption requires that companies say no to some things to conserve resources and ensure that remaining resources are focused on the right things.

But what specifically should companies say no to? Companies looking to shut down some innovation efforts have to evaluate two different portfolios: their portfolio of in-process innovation efforts and their portfolio of existing businesses (brands, product families, units, and so on). Prudently pruning these portfolios will help to ensure that resources flow to the right innovation efforts and to identify existing businesses that can be safely shed.

Managing In-process Innovations

Almost any sizable company has a number of in-process innovation efforts. Some of these efforts involve incremental improvements to existing products or services. Others involve efforts to bring existing offerings to new geographies or customer sets. Still others involve the creation of entirely new growth businesses. Well-run companies constantly monitor their innovation portfolio to determine which projects to accelerate, which to decelerate, and which to shut down.

The discussion that follows points out the flaws of two popular ways to prioritize innovation portfolios—focusing on first-year revenues and prioritizing projects based on net present value (NPV)—and suggests an alternative approach.

Approach 1: First-Year Revenues

Some companies will explicitly or implicitly prioritize projects based on their first-year revenues. In essence, this approach helps executives answer the question, "Where are my biggest ideas?" Obviously first-year revenues are important. But they are not the only thing that matter.

A good way to reinforce this notion is to ask a group of executives which of the following innovations they would prefer:

Innovation A. This innovation came out of the gates like a bullet, racking up first-year sales of more than $200 million. A clear value proposition, clever positioning, and a strong distribution network led to market success.

Innovation B. This innovation had first-year revenues of a mere $220,000. The innovation had cool technology, but no paying customers and an uncertain business model.

It's obvious, right? Innovation A is the winning proposition.

Let's reveal more information. Innovation A was Vanilla Coke. It was a line extension that largely cannibalized sales of the Coca-Cola Company's other products. Three years after launch, fizzling demand led the company to pull the product from the market.[1]

Innovation B was Google. In Google's early days, it had a technology and not much else. After a couple of iterations though, it came up with its advertising-based business model, setting the stage for one of the greatest economic success stories of current times.

Vanilla Cokes are great, but Googles are once in a lifetime. And the trick is that many great growth businesses start small and take a few years before they grow exponentially. We looked at twenty-two different disruptive businesses for which we could get complete data going back to the very first dollar of revenue. The set included some of the greatest growth businesses of our time, such as Google, Salesforce.com, and Netflix. The average first-year revenues of our data set? Less than $15 million. The businesses grew explosively after that first year, reaching an average of more than $200 million in their fourth year and $750 million by the sixth year (see figure 2-1). Companies that set astronomically high first-year bars would have killed these ideas and missed opportunities to create billions of dollars of value.

FIGURE 2-1

Revenue of disruptive companies by year

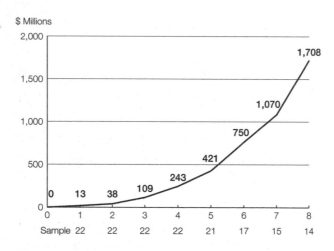

Note: Overall sample is 22 companies where data existed back to first year of revenues; figures not adjusted for inflation. Annual sample presents the number of companies from the overall sample in a given year.
Source: Thomson Financial; Compustat; Innosight Analysis.

Consider how Jeff Bezos from Amazon.com views this challenge:

> I am very proud of the senior team here because nobody on our team says, "Gosh, why are we paying any attention to this thing that may be growing fast but it is only 5 million in revenue?" If you want to be able to grow new trees you have to be able to plant small seeds and watch them grow into small saplings. What we do do, and I think it is very important, we do hold the new seeds to a standard. If they do work, and if they are successful they have to be able to grow into meaningful businesses, where meaningful is relative to the overall scale of Amazon.[2]

Approach 2: Net Present Value

Many companies make portfolio decisions based on the net present value of individual innovation efforts. That is, they project future cash flows, convert those future cash flows into present-day dollars using some discount rate, and prioritize the projects with the highest NPVs. In essence, this approach helps executives answer the question, "Which project is worth the most?"

The math behind NPV calculations is quite sensible, of course. And NPV seems to be an attractive way to compare different types of ideas. But the actual process many companies go through to make the calculations can be problematic.

One problem my colleague Clayton Christensen pointed out in a 2008 *Harvard Business Review* article: companies assume the "base case" is business as usual.[3] In reality, a company that doesn't innovate, particularly to respond to a disruptive threat in its market, faces declining prospects in its base business.

For example, consider a newspaper company deciding whether to invest in an online classified advertising offering. The company runs the analysis and concludes that the NPV is too low to warrant investment. But what happens if the company *doesn't* enter this market? Its core classified business would continue to erode in the face of significant competitive pressures.

Another problem is that companies often want to make decisions based on "the number" or a precise estimate of a project's potential. When companies only consider a single scenario, they almost always feel as if they have to be conservative, leading them to prioritize "sure things" in known markets over risky ventures in new markets.

While that approach might be reasonable when a company is launching a modest line extension into a known market, a new-to-the-world solution could unfold in infinite ways. It might be worth investing in a project that appears to have—on average—negative NPV if a modest investment can highlight whether outsized returns are possible (looking at investments in innovation as "options" is a technique that can be useful in this circumstance). Further, if you don't invest in the long term, you increase the odds that you will fall behind existing and emerging competitors in the next economic cycle. A company that rank-orders all of the projects in its innovation portfolio by NPV might unintentionally stop working on projects with the greatest long-term growth potential.

There are other problems that can lurk within many companies as well. Some companies have well-formulated templates to help simplify NPV calculations. Those templates almost always implicitly assume that an idea conforms to the company's current business model.

One consumer products company had a project blow up based on just such a hidden assumption. The project involved a device that was significantly more expensive than most of the company's products. Consumers would purchase the device and a consumable product that would work with it. The problem: consumers returned the high-priced devices with much greater frequency than they did the company's traditional products. As the returns flooded in, the financial projections collapsed.

If a company is using a new business model, some of the underlying assumptions about capital investment, margin structure, inventory turnover, and so on can be wildly different. A simplifying template can be a straitjacket for teams seeking to introduce new business models.

A Different Approach

It's natural to want to have a simple way to compare multiple projects quickly. But taking an overly simplistic approach can sometimes be the exact wrong thing to do. Any one approach is bound to have its flaws. Instead of focusing on a single metric, companies should consider the answers to the following five questions:

1. **What is the upside *potential*?** Of course, all things being equal, you would rather invest in a project that could produce huge returns than one that has limited upside potential. Make sure you run multiple scenarios and consider the "fringe" scenarios carefully. Is there any way a modest investment could identify whether huge returns are in fact a realistic possibility?

2. **How much risk remains?** Any project to be launched will have a degree of risk or uncertainty. Again, you should prefer a project with lower risk to one with more risk.

3. **What resources are required to reach the next learning milestone?** Ideally, companies can learn more about critical risks with modest incremental investment in time and dollars. A project with huge risk but huge potential might be worth keeping alive if you can learn about a critical unknown cheaply and quickly (discussed in more detail in chapter 5). The time frame matters a great deal—getting answers in six months is significantly better than getting answers in three years.

4. **How well does the idea fit a qualitative pattern of success?** Making decisions based purely on numbers that are nothing more than educated guesses is silly. Properly applied, qualitative metrics can be a useful way to

identify attractive opportunities early. For example, a consumer health care company used historical research to develop a twenty-point checklist for new at-home diagnostic ideas. That checklist helped the company to quickly screen nascent ideas.

5. **How much does the idea contribute to the overall portfolio's balance?** Modern portfolio theory suggests that reaching the ideal balance between risk and return means investing in assets that have noncorrelated risk. For innovation efforts, that might mean an approach to reach a new customer segment, use a new business model, or rely on different technologies. If companies don't consciously seek to diversify their innovation portfolios, they often end up with a narrow focus on near-in opportunities.

These kinds of questions can help companies identify when it is time to pull the plug on a project. When you can't shake residual risk, when tests grow increasingly expensive and learning increasingly scarce, and when it's getting harder to see the upside potential, it might be time to move on to another project. Making these decisions quickly can help companies maximize the return on their investments in innovation.

Our experience suggests that most innovation portfolios badly need this kind of assessment. Significant academic research shows how individual investors are better off by investing in diverse assets with uncorrelated risks. Executives carefully invest their own money in a wide range of stocks, bonds, and other assets to achieve this balance. Yet, most companies have shockingly undiversified innovation portfolios.

Well-run companies typically evaluate innovation portfolios on a regular rhythm, perhaps every 60, 90, 180, or 365 days. Significant market shifts, such as the economic shock of late 2008, are cause for off-cycle portfolio planning. Even companies that think they have a good handle on their innovation portfolio should ask questions such as:

- Do we have enough projects that, if half or more of them fail, we could still hit our revenue and profit targets?

- Which of the ideas should we accelerate, decelerate, or shut down?

- Do the projects in our portfolio have sufficiently different strategic intents?

"Tool 2-1: Portfolio checkup" at the end of this chapter provides questions to help companies evaluate their innovation portfolios.

A Side Benefit: Ungumming the Portfolio

One of our favorite stories about innovation involves a newspaper company's foray onto the Internet in the 1990s. Reflecting on the lessons learned from those efforts, the newspaper's editor said, "Given the pace of our expansion, I don't think we made mistakes fast enough and we didn't learn from them often enough. The problem wasn't just turning [the experiments] on, sometimes it was turning them off."[4]

Many leaders will say they simply don't have the capacity to innovate. When we look at their innovation pipeline, however, we notice something interesting. All innovation resources are allocated to existing projects, but many of those projects have been going on for years without much real progress. A couple of people still are toiling away, just in case. The resources are there, but people are spending time on efforts that are very unlikely to pay off. We call this a "zombie portfolio," full of "walking dead" projects (see "Portfolio Traps" for a more complete list of innovation portfolios to avoid).[5]

Companies that prudently prune their portfolio of in-process innovations can find that they have more innovation resources at their disposal than they realized—resources that could be redeployed to go after the sorts of high-potential opportunities described in subsequent chapters.

Pruning Existing Businesses

One of the least heralded tasks of the world-class innovator is the dispassionate disposal of businesses that have passed the corporate equivalent of a sell-by date. But moving out of old markets is as important as moving into new markets, particularly for companies seeking to transform themselves.

Clearly the need to exit businesses becomes more acute when times are tough and budgets are slim. Continuing to focus on increasingly off-strategy and underperforming

PORTFOLIO TRAPS

- **An "open door" portfolio.** This portfolio features limited investment in the base business and significant investment in unrelated or semirelated diversification. This type of portfolio often results from the incorrect assumption that a healthy core business will remain healthy in perpetuity. As competitors encroach on the core business, diversification efforts inevitably get deprioritized as the company hunkers down and focuses on defending the core.

- **A "zero-sum" portfolio.** This portfolio features large investments in revenue-generating extensions to existing platforms and limited investments in truly new growth initiatives. This type of portfolio might succeed in protecting a platform from attack, but it offers limited upside potential because a company is essentially shifting profit from one of its products to another.

- **A "zombie" portfolio.** This portfolio has investment in a wide range of innovation initiatives that appeared, at least on formulation, to have potential. However, a stark look at many of the initiatives reveals that the true level of upside potential is lower than initial projections, yet no mechanisms are in place to reallocate resources away from the least-promising initiatives. As a result, resources remain committed to walking dead ("zombie") initiatives that will generate a fractional return on investment at best.

- **A "plain vanilla" portfolio.** This portfolio features investment in a single type of innovation (e.g., product feature improvement). Innovation portfolios that do not include a wide variety of types of innovations (e.g., category creation, business model) can leave substantial sums of money on the table.

businesses takes not only scare resources but even scarcer management time.

The natural tendency is to let past performance guide the discussion. One popular approach is the Boston Consulting Group's growth-share matrix. That framework suggests riding "stars" with high share in a fast-growing market, milking "cows" with high share in low-growth markets, shooting "dogs" with low share in low-growth markets, and examining the "questions" with low share in high-growth markets.[6]

Past performance is a natural place to turn, because companies can gather data about the past. After all, reliable data about the future doesn't exist. Past data helps to explain what *has happened*. However, it does not always provide a reasonable assessment of what *will happen*. Of course, in highly stable circumstances, past data can be a strong indicator of future performance. The Great Disruption is anything but stable, however. The gales of creative destruction have never blown more fiercely. Technology changes happen seemingly overnight. Competitors can spring up from distant geographies or from seemingly unconnected industries.

Companies making decisions based on past data can miss important trends that portend massive changes in their core market. They can shed the very assets that will be critical components of future success, even though the past performance has disappointed.

For example, step back to 1994. Imagine you are a senior executive of the Washington Post Company. Investors are pressuring you to boost the company's profits. You decide it is a good time to take stock of your portfolio of businesses. You are pretty happy with your core printing and publishing business. In 1994 newspapers like the *Washington Post* and magazines like *Newsweek* provided more than $1.1 billion in revenues and $150 million in operating income. Both figures had grown steadily over the past few years. On the other hand, an acquisition you made in 1984 just wasn't working out. That part of the business provided revenues of about $150 million and lost close to $25 million. Revenues were growing slowly—always a bad sign for a relatively small unit—and losses had increased by about $15 million from the previous year.

The past data suggests you should consider shedding the low-performing business unit to focus on your core. Fortunately, the Washington Post Company decided to keep investing in its new growth business—educational services provider Kaplan. The company brought in a new executive team for the unit, and growth accelerated dramatically. In

2007, traditional newspapers and magazines reported revenues of about $1.2 billion, with net profits of about $100 million. Kaplan had become a $2 billion business that contributed $150 million in operating income.

As every mutual fund prospectus states, "Past performance is no guarantee of future results." When making forward-looking decisions, companies need to make decisions based not just on *performance,* but on *potential* as well. To determine the market potential of a brand, division, or business unit, companies should look at the current potential still left to exploit in existing markets and option value to create or enter new markets. Evaluating these two factors can help companies to determine which brands, product families, or business units require disproportionate investment, and which should be deemphasized or even shut down. While there is a significant amount of art in using the approach described next, the structured line of thinking can help companies make the right strategic decisions.

Unexploited Potential

The first factor to examine is the unexploited potential a brand, product line, division, or company has for profitable expansion within current markets. For example, as of 2008, Google still had unexploited potential in its core advertising market. The company's staggering growth from 1998 to 2008 makes it easy to forget that most companies still rely largely on traditional forms of media, such as print and television. Further, many small businesses don't advertise at all. As Google continues to improve its offering and more and more companies get comfortable advertising online, the company is in good position to drive continued growth.

On the other hand, how much room for continued growth does the Coca-Cola Company's Coke brand have? The brand's global ubiquity, coupled with fierce competition from global and local players, means that the Coca-Cola Company simply can't count on its flagship brand to drive future growth.

Four specific analyses can help to determine the degree to which an existing business has unexploited potential:

1. **Up-market potential.** This analysis seeks to understand how much room there is to improve current offerings to reach current or more-demanding customers. What percent of the total addressable market has been penetrated? How easy is it to reach other parts of the market? The more room and ability there is to march up-market, the greater the exploitation potential.

2. **S-curve position.** If you map how a technology improves over time, it almost always follows a pattern resembling an *S*. That is, after steady but slow improvement, at some point scientists figure out how to improve performance rapidly before they hit a technological wall and the rate of improvement slows again. The position of a current business on the S curve indicates the required investment to achieve the performance improvements required to realize up-market potential.[7]

3. **Competitive advantage.** Classic competitive strategy can help determine the degree to which the company is in a good position to seize whatever potential might exist in the market. Of course, never assume that competitive advantage is stable; rather, it is important to understand who will have competitive advantage over the next time period.

4. **Emerging disruptors.** The more companies that are following disruptive approaches have taken root in and around an existing market, the more difficult it will be for incumbent companies to realize profitable growth. Watch specifically for companies that intentionally trade off performance to achieve lower prices. *Seeing What's Next*, a 2004 book I coauthored with Harvard Business School Professor Clayton Christensen, details a number of analyses to identify whether a potential disruptor has taken root and whether it has a good chance of driving disruptive growth.[8]

To sum up, unexploited potential is high when market penetration is low, driving improvements is achievable and affordable, a company has defensible sources of competitive advantage, and the market is relatively free of disruptors poised to change the game and suck profits out of the industry.

Option Value

The next factor to assess is the degree to which a brand, product line, division, or company can create profitable growth in *other* markets. In other words, is there some kind of unique asset that could open up growth in another market?

A good example of a company with high degrees of hidden option value is Wal-Mart. The company's low-cost operations and wide retail footprint presents a powerful platform to disrupt other markets. Historically the company's growth has been driven by successive moves into white goods, clothing, groceries, and so on. As of this writing, Wal-Mart was exploring opportunities to compete in health care and financial services.

On the other hand, a company like Delta has relatively few assets that could enable it to move into other markets. The specialized skills it has built to compete in the aviation market allow it to be a formidable competitor in that market, but its ability to grow into new markets is relatively low.

Determining option value involves detailing a company's full complement of assets—brand equity, technology, capabilities, relationships, and so on—and assessing whether those assets could transfer to adjacent markets or be used to create new markets. When making this assessment, companies need to walk a delicate balance. They need to think about the capabilities they have that they can legitimately leverage to create new growth. But they have to remember how Harvard Business School Professor Howard Stevenson defines entrepreneurship: the pursuit of opportunity without regard to resources controlled.

Strategic Implications

Figure 2-2 summarizes the implication of assessing unexploited potential and option value. When current potential is

FIGURE 2-2

Assessing unexploited potential and option value

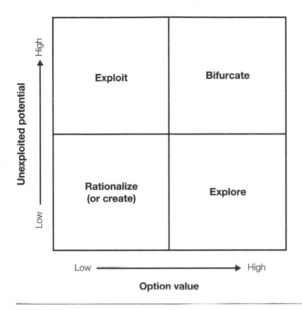

high and option value is low, companies should seek to *exploit* the potential of their innovation. They should seal up competitive advantage through improving existing offerings to better appeal to current customers and more-demanding customers. The focus is on playing the game better than other market competitors. Google has appropriately been in exploitation mode in its core search-based advertising business over the past five years. Its core focus has been on improving its targeting capability, finding ways to improve its search algorithm, and increasing the amount of advertising inventory it has so it can get more money from existing advertisers and reach new ones.

When unexploited potential is low and option value seems high, companies should *explore* to confirm which strategy has the most potential (and then, of course, exploit that potential). Exploration involves looking for ways to change the game in current markets, expand into markets that exist but are new to the company, or create entirely new categories of growth. Exploration efforts often start rather modestly until a company figures out a strategy that will drive transformative growth. If it turns out that the new markets are not substantial enough, companies should consider exiting the business.

When both factors are high, companies need to split or *bifurcate* their efforts so exploitation doesn't squeeze out exploration and vice versa.

Finally, when both potential and option value are low, companies should *rationalize* current efforts by managing for cash, shutting the business down, or selling the business off. Any investment should focus on process improvements or cost innovations that improve the business unit's overall profit profile. For example, while it has been painful for frequent fliers, major airlines that have cut back on frills, consolidated routes, and sought operating efficiencies have followed a sensible strategy given their circumstances.

Of course, if *all* of a company's businesses are in the lower-left quadrant, the company has to build new assets that can help it to create new growth businesses.

Example Application

After years of mediocre performance in one of its business units, a manufacturer of branded durable consumer goods took a hard look at the offerings in the unit's portfolio. The company faced a fiercely competitive market, and some of its brands seemed to offer little differentiated value to the consumer. The company started by conducting deep market research to understand how the *consumer* experienced the category. That research served as input into tough decisions about brands to maintain, change, and shed, and new brands to create.

Several counterintuitive findings came from the analysis. Some items in the portfolio that provided the greatest historical profits weren't the ones with the greatest future potential because of increased competition and shifting consumer demand. The company planned to discontinue some of these brands to free up resources for other efforts. Some of the brands that appeared to be stagnating were actually "hidden gems," where directed investment could create highly differentiated offerings. The company also uncovered nonobvious ways to reposition existing products to more closely connect with a particular group of consumers. Finally, in what seemed to be a stagnant, commoditized category, the company pinpointed an opportunity to create a completely new platform of products based on simplicity that could attract new consumers into the category. The three-month effort created a multiyear innovation road map for the business unit.

Tips on Divesting

If you decide you have to divest a business, what is the best way to do it? This is a natural question for companies that do not have deep experience with divestitures. And getting this question right can have big impact. Three partners from Bain & Company analyzed more than seven thousand divestures over a twenty-year period and found that the best divestors significantly outperformed the sample.[9] As an example, the Bain trio cited Weyerhaeuser, a forest-products company that has divested close to $10 billion dollars of businesses since 2004. It used the proceeds from those divestitures to help transition from commodity pulp-and-paper businesses to more value-added materials and real estate.

In a 2008 *Harvard Business Review* article, the Bain partners detailed four rules for companies seeking to become world class at divesting:

1. Dedicate a full-time divestment team.

2. Establish objective criteria (such as the ones discussed earlier) to determine divestment candidates.

3. Work through the process of divestiture—before you decide to divest.

4. Ensure you can articulate how the deal will help the buyer and how you can motivate employees to stay on after the divestiture.[10]

Following these four tips can help companies maximize their ability to successfully execute divestitures.

A Good Discipline

The discipline from following the approaches described in this chapter should serve a company in good times or bad.

Innovation is more predictable and less random than many perceive. But it is still reasonable to assume that you will fail more often than you will succeed. As such, prudently pruning the innovation portfolio can help ensure that you are efficiently allocating resources to the best ideas.

In addition, shedding business units, brands, or product lines is a critical part of the process of creative destruction. Research by Innosight board member Richard Foster shows how almost all companies underperform broader market indexes over any substantial period of time.[11] One reason for this result, Foster argues, is that companies that survive are excellent operators, whereas markets feature substantial creation of new companies and destruction of old companies.

To outperform the market then, Foster argues that companies have to change at the pace of the market, without losing control. The discipline of looking at the portfolio of operating businesses on a regular basis can help companies function more like the market, increasing the ability to generate above-average returns.

The evaluations described in this chapter should be part of the ongoing strategic review process. For example, every year Procter & Gamble has its individual business units map out their growth strategies. Those that cannot develop reasonable plans to hit minimum corporate guidelines become targets for disposal. Over the past decade, P&G has sold off brands such as ThermaCare, Jif, Crisco, and Folgers. In late 2008, the company decided to decrease investment in developing its own pharmaceutical products so it could focus more on consumer health care brands like Vicks.

The Great Disruption means that discussions about decelerating or exiting businesses need to happen on a more frequent basis. Companies need to regularly take a hard look at their broad portfolio and make tough choices before their hands are tied.

Summary

Continuing to prioritize innovation efforts in recessionary periods requires strong senior leadership. The overwhelming tendency is to slash resources, shut down long-term investments, and focus on incremental improvements. Taking the wrong actions can sharply inhibit a company's ability to reach its long-term strategic objectives. Approaching the problem in the right way can allow companies to do more with less and continue to move forward in appropriate ways.

This chapter described how to prudently prune the innovation portfolio. Specifically, it suggested:

- Companies need to think about evaluating two portfolios: in-process innovation efforts and existing brands, product families, business units, or divisions.

- The usual techniques companies use—focusing on first-year revenue or NPV figures for in-process innovations or past performance for broader units—can lead to strategic mistakes.

- Companies should look at five factors when looking at in-process innovations: upside potential, residual risk, required near-term investment, fit with qualitative patterns, and unique contribution to portfolio balance.

- When evaluating businesses, companies should look at the degree to which the unit has unexploited potential in existing markets and option value to create or enter new markets. Businesses that lack both potential and option value are candidates for disposal.

TOOL 2-1

Portfolio checkup

The following questions can help to determine the health of your innovation/growth portfolio. The beginner questions are intended for people who are just starting to formulate their portfolio; the advanced questions are intended for people who already have a good handle on the basics of their portfolio.

Beginner

1. Do you have a list of every innovation project your company is working on?
2. Does that list include basic information about each project, such as time to launch, upside potential, key risks, near-term activities, committed human resources, and required investment?
3. Does your portfolio have a risk-adjusted expected value?
4. Do you have a target return for your portfolio?
5. If half of your projects fail, will you still be able to reach your growth objectives?
6. Do you have guidelines for target investment by stage in your innovation process?

Advanced

1. Do you have separate portfolios for ideas with meaningfully different strategic intents?
2. Do you know what the profile of an idea in each portfolio looks like?
3. Do you consciously seek to invest in projects that are uncorrelated with the rest of the portfolio along meaningful strategic dimensions?
4. Do you use option thinking to understand the potential of individual projects?
5. Do you have approaches to shed declining businesses to create space for new growth?
6. Do you have a process to regularly refresh and review your portfolio?

Refeature to Cut Costs

In the late 1890s, soup consumption was close to nonexistent
because shipping was too expensive. Campbell's condensed
soup sacrificed quality but lowered prices by 70 percent.
You can, in fact, do more with less if you approach
cost cutting in the right way.

The previous chapter described things a company should
stop doing. This chapter and the three that follow discuss
what companies need to *do differently* in a tough economic
climate.

In tough times, it's common for leaders to implore their
companies to figure out how to do "more with less." It's a
nice thing to say, but *how* exactly can a company do more
with less? This chapter describes how to intelligently
refeature existing products and services to cut costs. Core

disruptive principles can help companies meet bottom-line profit targets *and* realize growth opportunities they might otherwise miss.

Cost-Cutting Lessons from Disruptive Innovation

Cost cutting can be very dangerous. Haphazard cost cutting can lead companies to unintentionally damage their ability to serve today's customers and destroy their ability to create tomorrow's growth businesses. Constant cost cutting can damage morale and make it difficult for people to focus on the business at hand.

During tough times, it is not unusual for companies to issue broad mandates that all divisions cut a certain percentage of their budgets. But these mandates offer precious little guidance about *how* exactly divisions should achieve those cost savings. Should a company start using cheaper material? Strip out bells and whistles? Lower salesforce incentives? Reduce administrative head count? Take a little from everything (so-called "peanut butter" cuts)?

Understanding the drivers of disruptive innovation—a time-tested path to growth described in chapter 1—provides a way to think differently about feature reduction and cost cutting. Harvard Business School professor Clayton Christensen's original research on disruptive innovation found that the best-run companies would fail in the face of a disruptive attack. The reason for this failure wasn't managerial incompetence or poor execution. Rather, companies would fail when a competitor introduced a product that was *worse* than the product offered by leading incumbents, at least along dimensions of performance that historically mattered to mainstream customers.[1]

The disruptive offering wasn't bad. It crossed a threshold that made it good enough along traditional dimensions and traded off pure performance to achieve greater simplicity, convenience, or low prices. The disruptor didn't target the most-demanding customers in a market. Rather, the disruptor found a happy home among customers who couldn't use or didn't want to pay for all the performance of existing solutions, or people who faced a constraint that inhibited their ability to consume existing solutions. As a disruptor improved its offering, it would cross performance thresholds that would allow it to compete in more demanding market tiers, where its superior simplicity and affordability served as sources of competitive advantage.

A classic example of disruptive innovation is the personal computer. In the early days, the personal computer could not do much. But it was simpler and cheaper than existing minicomputers. Early consumers used personal computers to play games, balance their checkbooks, and do simple word processing. As personal computers improved, they crossed performance thresholds that made them viable for corporate tasks, and companies flocked to the devices. Minicomputer titans such as Digital Equipment Corporation, Prime Computer, Wang, and Nixdorf Computer crumbled as personal computer manufacturers such as Compaq, Hewlett-Packard, Apple, and Dell soared.

Southwest Airlines is another disruptive poster child. It intentionally traded off frills for affordability. Of course, it crosses basic thresholds for safety and performance. But a strategy based on cost has given Southwest Airlines defensible competitive advantage for thirty years.

Why are incumbent firms susceptible to disruption? One reason is that in pursuit of profits in the high end of their respective industries, these companies end up providing too much performance for many groups of consumers. The disruptive literature calls this "overshooting" (a concept that is described in more depth in chapter 7). Also, companies can lack a fundamental understanding of a customer's performance thresholds and tolerable trade-offs. Engineers might denigrate a simple solution as being not good enough, but that simple solution could be the key to market success.

The basic pattern of disruptive innovation has three important lessons for cost cutting:

1. Different customers define quality differently. Some customers care deeply about raw performance; others focus on convenience or cost.

2. A company has to cross a "good enough" threshold to compete in a given market tier.

3. Disruptors master the art of trade-offs, intentionally sacrificing raw performance in the name of convenience, simplicity, or affordability.

The following discussion details how to use these lessons as part of a three-step process to drive intelligent cost cutting. First, segment your market by the jobs customers are trying to get done. Then, determine the thresholds and trade-offs different segments have along various performance dimensions. Finally, consider how you can get the customer's job done in a way that meets your cost objectives.

It is important to reiterate that this process isn't really about *cost cutting*; it is about *refeaturing* to really get a customer's job done. As such, the process described is also critical for innovators that are developing completely new offerings.

Step 1: Segment Markets

Almost any established company has some way to segment its market. A company that sells to consumers might consider basic demographic demarcations (males over thirty-five) or more psychographic or needs-based markers ("beauty seekers"). A company that sells to other businesses might classify customers based on their geography, annual revenues, or industry.

These segmentation schemes help companies to organize data about their markets and to advertise and distribute their goods and services appropriately. Our experience, however, is that the segments end up not being particularly useful guides to innovation.

As Christensen noted in the foreword to our 2008 book *The Innovator's Guide to Growth*:

> Product and customer characteristics are poor indicators of customer behavior, because from the customer's perspective that is not how markets are structured. Customers' purchase decisions don't necessarily conform to those of the "average" customer in their

demographic; nor do they confine the search for solutions within a product category.

When customers find that they need to get a job done, they hire products or services to do the job. This means that companies need to understand the jobs that arise in customers' lives for which their products might be hired. In other words, the job, and not the customer or the product, should be the fundamental unit of market segmentation and analysis.

Most of the "home runs" of marketing history were hit by marketers who sensed the fundamental job that customers were trying to get done—and then found a way to help more people get it done more effectively, conveniently and affordably. The strike-outs of marketing history, in contrast, generally have been the result of developing products with better features and functions than other products in the same category, or of attempting to decipher what the average customer in a demographic wants. Working to understand the job to be done is worth the effort.[2]

The most actionable way to segment a market is to develop a deep understanding of the target customer's *job-to-be-done,* the *circumstances* in which they encounter that job, the performance *objectives* that the customer considers important, the *barriers* that inhibit the customer's ability to get the job done, and the *solutions* that the customer considers.

Here's a definition of each italicized term in the previous paragraph.[3]

Job-to-be-done. A problem that a given customer is trying to solve. Christensen introduced the concept of jobs-to-be-done in *The Innovator's Solution.* In that book, he famously described how customers hire fast-food milkshakes for nonobvious reasons, such as providing companionship during long, boring commutes.[4] The single most important question for determining if you have a legitimate job-to-be-done is to ask "Why?" When the answer to the "Why?" question is "Because!" you have discovered a fundamental job-to-be-done. For example, having straight hair is not a job. It is a benefit. A customer might want to have straight hair so that she can be confident when she is giving an important internal presentation.

Circumstances. A variable that has an impact on performance objectives, barriers, and possible solutions. Location is an obvious circumstance. Life stage is another one. Consumer products companies need to consider a customer's emotional or mental state. A company's stage of growth would be an important circumstance for companies that sell to businesses.

Objectives. Metrics that customers use to determine whether or not a solution gets a job done in a particular circumstance (discussed in more detail later).

Barriers. Factors that inhibit a customer's ability to get a job done in a particular circumstance. Barriers tend to be related to skills, wealth, access, time, or knowledge.

Solutions. Products and services the customer considers and behaviors the customer follows to get the job done. The customer's solution set almost always looks wider than products that populate a particular category. For example, a consumer looking to rewear garments could use perfume to cover up odors, chose an outdoor venue where malodor is less noticeable, or use Swash, a line of sprays and other products Procter & Gamble introduced in 2007 to help facilitate confident rewear. Behaviors are often hidden competitors for a customer's job-to-be-done.

Traditional market research tools—focus groups, ethnographic research, quantitative surveys, and so on—can help to develop deeper insight into each of these elements and highlight rich ways to segment a market.

For example, one medical device company used the approach to understand customers of oral appliances, like aligners and orthodontic equipment. Historically, it assumed that major customer categories were general practitioners and specialists. Further, it assumed that the most critical jobs-to-be-done related to patient care.

The company was surprised to learn that many customers also cared a great deal about the business side of their practice and in projecting a certain image to other professionals. Beyond patient care, they cared about more efficient marketing, streamlined operations, and ways to minimize the time it took to learn about new devices.

This understanding opened up previously obscured innovation levers like training and inventory management and highlighted a more effective way to segment markets by looking at a practitioner's experience and passion about the business side of his or her practice. The company separated dentists that were generally seeking to "expand skills" from those that were focused on "getting started" or "running a business." The company could peg a dentist into one of these categories largely by the cumulative number of surgical procedures performed and the size of the practice.

Step 2: Determine Thresholds and Tolerable Trade-offs

After identifying meaningful segments, drill into how customers within each segment think about performance objectives or the metrics they use to choose between different solutions.

There are three basic categories of performance objectives:

1. Functional objectives, which relate to performance and reliability. Examples of functional objectives include "removes at least 95 percent of stains," "charges in less than an hour," "works every time," "requires no training."

2. Emotional objectives, which typically are things that customers feel about themselves. Examples of emotional objectives include "treat myself to the best," "connect me with others," "feel like I got good value."

3. Social objectives, which typically are things the customer perceives that others feel about them.

> Examples of social objectives include, "impress my peers," "reflect my personal brand," "withstand the withering glare of the 'mom police.'"

Companies should then understand which of these objectives are most important to the customer, what thresholds *have* to be crossed to enter into the customer's decision set, and what trade-offs the customer would *tolerate* between objectives. In other words, what's absolutely necessary, and what would a customer be willing to sacrifice?

Evaluating the performance offered by the lowest-priced, lowest-quality product on the market provides a good starting point for threshold performance; market research can provide more robust data on thresholds and tolerable trade-offs. One popular approach is conjoint analysis. This technique involves showing customers a number of paired product comparisons with different feature and functionality bundles. By comparing multiple pairs and using advanced statistical techniques, a company can determine how much value a customer places on each feature.

A simpler approach involves asking survey respondents to rate whether randomly selected performance characteristics meet, exceed, or fail to meet expectations. While the results are not as statistically valid as conjoint analysis, they can help companies understand the dividing line between "good enough" and "not good enough" performance, and "good enough" and "too good" performance.

A related technique is known as *Kano* (so named for its originator Noriaki Kano, who developed the technique at the Tokyo University of Science in the late 1970s). Kano techniques involve asking customers how they would feel if they received a particular benefit, and how they would feel if they did *not* receive that benefit. Kano techniques help to separate "delighters" (factors that would "wow" a customer because they don't expect it) from "must haves" (where customers expect a certain threshold performance, but don't value much beyond the threshold) and "linear satisfiers" (where satisfaction moves in lockstep with performance).

Step 3: Refeature Offerings

The knowledge about thresholds and trade-offs then serve as critical inputs into how to change current offerings. The trick is to ensure that you cross the basic performance threshold on every critical dimension, then *selectively* overperform in areas that provide the most customer value while thoughtfully *decreasing* performance along dimensions that don't matter a great deal to a given customer group (see "Bottom-up Cost Cutting" for a slightly different approach).

For example, one cement company separated customers seeking strong concrete for support columns from those seeking more "workable" concrete to put into walls and staircases. It also separated customers seeking high service from those looking for "just the basics" at low prices. Instead of providing a one-size-fits-none solution, the company introduced distinct offerings for each segment. The result? Each segment became larger and more profitable. That's more with less![5]

BOTTOM-UP COST CUTTING

Companies typically conduct cost cutting from the top down. Another approach is to start from the ground up. What fixed and variable costs are required to hit the minimum performance thresholds for the business? What markups and margins do the company, channel, and other partners require? This build-up activity sets the minimum price tag to compete in a marketplace. Then the company can choose which features it wants to invest in to create competitive advantage. Surprisingly, this approach can result in coming in under the budget target, while creating an offering that connects more comprehensively with customers.

Some specific areas that companies should consider include:

Raw material. The analysis might highlight that certain raw materials providing gold-standard performance lead to performance differences that are imperceptible to the customer. Maybe you can use less raw material or find a completely different way to produce your product.

Sales staff. It is possible that some customers don't value an intimate sales process with substantial hand holding. For example, small businesses looking to find a simple way to manage their customer contacts don't want to deal with a complicated, customized pitch from a company like Oracle. They'd rather use simple solutions from

Salesforce.com, 37signals, or NetSuite that they can obtain and begin using quickly and easily.

Postsales support. Companies can expend significant amounts of money providing the exact wrong kind of postsales support to customers. While some customers undoubtedly want human interaction when they have a problem, many want the ability to find precise answers to their questions quickly and see how other customers have solved similar problems. Cisco Systems, for example, has created online forums where customers can learn from other customers.

Features. Maybe there is a whiz-bang feature in your product that doesn't matter that much to a particular customer set. For example, many newspaper companies have reduced or combined sections of the newspaper or moved away from daily publishing. The readers who miss particular features can still find the information online, and the companies can save on printing and distribution.

Marketing. Generally, our perspective is that much of a company's investment in marketing is a waste—particularly for young companies that feel pressure to build brands. One of the dot.com eras' biggest flameouts, Pets.com, invested tens of millions of dollars building a brand when it had a shaky business model and no real source of competitive advantage. Its sock puppet is still widely recognized today, but the company shut down more than six years ago. After all, how did commonplace brands like Google, Amazon.com, and others become commonplace? It wasn't through massive advertising investments. Rather, the elegant simplicity of these companies' offerings led customers to recommend the products to their friends. As Intuit founder and chairman Scott Cook puts it, "One of the biggest drivers of new brand trial, and thus new brand reputation building, is word of mouth. And friends tell their friends about the product or service. They don't generally tell them about advertising."[6]

Taking a hard look at thresholds and trade-offs can lead companies to realize that they've been allocating investment to things that just aren't meaningful to important customer segments. Not only can following this approach allow intelligent refeaturing to maintain or improve profitability, it can illuminate new ways to appeal to previously hard-to-reach customer groups. The right kind of cost cutting can put a company back into consideration by a customer segment that previously deemed the solution to be too expensive. Or, companies can find ways to make their products simple enough to connect with a group of customers who considered the solution too complicated.

A historical example of growth through intelligent refeaturing in difficult economic conditions comes from Campbell's introduction of condensed soup in the late 1890s. At the time, soup was very cheap to make, but very perishable and expensive to ship. John Dorrance, a twenty-four-year-old nephew of the Joseph Campbell Preserve Co.'s general manager, had the innovative idea of reducing half of the soup's water to make it last longer and cheaper to ship. It wasn't as simple as removing water. Dorrance drew on his knowledge of chemistry to figure out how to create a strong stock that would hold its flavor when the consumer added water to reconstitute the stock. In the late 1890s, Campbell's introduced tomato, consommé, vegetable, chicken, and oxtail soups. Dorrance's innovative refeaturing—sacrificing quality and consumer choice for portability and price—slashed the price of soup from 30 cents per 32-ounce can to 10 cents per 10-ounce can. Dorrance sold his soup stock door-to-door to convince skeptical Americans that soup could become an affordable part of their daily diet. Capitalizing on Dorrance's innovation made the company profitable for the first time, and in 1921 the company renamed itself the Campbell Soup Company.[7]

This approach also helps to identify hidden innovation levers that can create space between a company and its competitors. The medical device company mentioned earlier invested heavily in training, inventory management, and other forms of postsales support to help dentists better manage their business. It provided assistance in building market awareness of its device's advantages over alternative treatment approaches, created tools that allowed dentists to communicate the device's functionality to patients, and thought of new mechanisms to help patients pay for the treatment. By pulling these and other innovation levers, the company was able to more sharply differentiate itself against its competitors. Eighteen months after the company embarked on its innovation efforts, its major competitor had gone bankrupt.

What About Internal Processes?

Most of this chapter focused on how to think about cutting the costs that are directly related to the production or delivery of a specific product or service. What about cutting corporate overhead? How should an office manager who has to cut 20 percent of her budget approach the problem?

The notion of thresholds and trade-offs continues to provide useful guidance, even if the customer of a particular function is internal. What do internal customers absolutely require, and what can they live without? Is there an innovative way to organize internal functions to deliver similar value at radically lower prices? Many companies outsource key functions based on similar analysis. They recognize that they might lose the ability to receive customized, on-demand service, but are happy to trade that off for lower costs or the flexibility to quickly scale services up or down, based on business conditions.

Companies can also use this line of thinking to intelligently reduce benefits for their staff. Companies often provide one-size-fits-all benefits, but understanding what really matters to staff can allow companies to unbundle benefits in ways that maintain employee morale and sharply lower costs. Tough times can lead to different compensation models. For example, toy company Fisher-Price (now a unit of Mattel) was founded by Herman Fisher, Ian Price, and his wife in the frigid economic climate of 1930. The company paid very low wages, but promised employees a stake of future profits—an early precursor of the boom in equity compensation over the past three decades. The company distributed $3,000 worth of silver dollars to employees when it earned its first profits in 1936.[8]

Summary

When times get tough, innovators have to figure out how to improve the productivity and profitability of existing products, services, and processes. Cost cutting is rarely a fun activity. But thoughtful approaches can actually result in reconstituted offerings that provide *better* value in the eyes of external and internal customers.

The basic principle of disruptive innovation shows how different customer groups define quality in different ways. Understanding thresholds of performance that must be crossed and tolerable trade-offs to customers can help guide cost-cutting efforts. Specifically, companies should follow a three-step process where they:

1. Segment customers using the concept of jobs-to-be-done.

2. Investigate discrete customer segments to determine thresholds and trade-offs.

3. Refeature offerings so they are more aligned with customer demand.

4

Increase Innovation Productivity

Historically, companies have had innovation batting averages that wouldn't qualify them for a cellar-dwelling baseball team. The right strategies, processes, systems, and structures can help companies compete in the innovation big leagues.

The previous chapter described how to improve the productivity of preexisting products, services, and processes. This chapter discusses how companies can improve the productivity of broader efforts to create new products, services, and processes by developing strategies, structures, and processes to improve their innovation success rate.

Improving that success rate is a pressing challenge. Ted Williams was one of the greatest baseball hitters who ever lived. His lifetime .344 batting average is the seventh highest of all time, and the highest of any player born after 1900. He once said, "Baseball is the only field of endeavor where a man can succeed three times out of ten and be considered a good performer." Williams obviously never tried to create a new growth business, where success rates of 20 to 25 percent are not uncommon.

This chapter draws on the concepts in *The Innovator's Guide to Growth* (a 2008 book written by me, two colleagues from Innosight, and an executive from Motorola) to describe how to dramatically boost that innovation "batting average."[1] It describes how to get ready for innovation, details a simple process to create booming new growth businesses, and provides guidance for how to embed innovation capabilities within your organization (see figure 4-1).

Getting Ready for Innovation

Imagine that you are a fifty-year-old male who has let his health deteriorate. You are overweight and can't find a way to fit exercise into your everyday routine. Then one day a friend calls you up and says, "Let's run the Boston Marathon together." Would you sign up? Of course not. You simply aren't ready for that level of competition.

Similarly, it is critical that companies make sure they are ready for innovation. It's not as easy as it sounds. Many companies have spent the past two decades focusing on operational effectiveness. Innovation muscles at many corporations have atrophied.

FIGURE 4-1

How to boost your innovation batting average

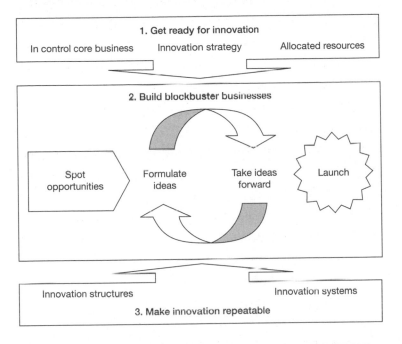

Source: Scott D. Anthony, Mark W. Johnson, Joseph V. Sinfield, and Elizabeth J. Altman, *The Innovator's Guide to Growth: Putting Disruptive Innovation to Work* (Boston: Harvard Business Press, 2008).

Getting ready for innovation involves three actions: gaining control over your core business, defining your innovation strategy, and allocating resources to realize that strategy. Let's start with gaining control over your core business. What exactly does that mean? Generally speaking, when your core business is in control you are rarely surprised by financial performance. Your revenues and profits show at least average growth for your industry. And you don't regularly scramble to respond to innovations launched by competitors.

Note, this does not mean that your core business must be thriving. Sometimes your core business will be in structural decline, and that's fine—as long as you are managing that decline in a way that minimizes surprises that are sure to pull you away from any innovation efforts.

If your core business is in control, turn next to your innovation strategy. Companies that are just starting their innovation efforts often begin by getting a group of people together and telling them, "It's innovation time!" These efforts rarely succeed.

Instead, create an innovation strategy that details clear targets and tactics. Targets help internal innovators know what they are shooting for. A reasonable starting place is to imagine what success looks like five years in the future. Are you seeking to double your business? Hold it steady? Something else?

Then think about the sources of growth. How much can you reasonably expect your core business to contribute? What contribution can you reasonably expect from what is already in your development pipeline? One tip here: make sure to adjust your pipeline for risk. If you assume all of your projects will succeed, you are being wildly optimistic. Finally, calculate the gap (and it will almost always be a gap) between where your projections suggest your business will be and where you want it to be. That gap is your target for new innovation efforts.

One cable broadcaster conducted a gap-calculating exercise in late 2006 on the heels of record-breaking financial performance. The company had all its executives come up with a set of reasonable estimates for key variables that drove the financial performance of the business. It had executives detail what were plausible ranges for each of those variables. It fed the ranges into a simple model and found that there was a frighteningly high chance that it could miss projected earnings by hundreds of millions of dollars, an event that would have devastating consequences. The effort helped to spur the company to bolster its innovation efforts.

After gaining alignment on the targets, detail tactical choices that are on and off the table. A lot of people think that creativity and chaos are friends. They aren't. The best way to spur innovation is to carefully consider what you definitely want innovators to do, what you'll consider, and what you definitely *don't* want innovators to do.

One way to make the tactical options tangible is to fill in figure 4-2. The figure represents goals and boundaries for innovation efforts. Note how the figure includes a diverse set of elements, such as steady-state revenue, revenue source, distribution channel, and brand. Customize the vectors for your context and gain consensus about what's clearly in bounds, what's on the fringes, and what's clearly out of bounds.

Finally, make sure you have allocated sufficient resources to bring your strategy to life. Innovation doesn't happen by accident. People have to spend time and, of course, money nurturing new growth efforts.

Generally, companies make two mistakes when allocating resources for innovation. First, they underestimate the importance of fully dedicated human resources. In most

FIGURE 4-2

How to determine your goals and boundaries

Source: Scott D. Anthony, Mark W. Johnson, Joseph V. Sinfield, and Elizabeth J. Altman, *The Innovator's Guide to Growth: Putting Disruptive Innovation to Work* (Boston: Harvard Business Press, 2008).

companies, asking everyone to spend a little bit of time on innovation is a good way to guarantee that no one spends time on innovation. After all, how much attention do people pay to the twelfth item on their to-do list? (As one colleague quipped, a 5 percent commitment is the equivalent of two lunches a week.) Companies often complain that they lack the money to innovate, but in reality, you can almost always find the money if you need it. Adding a twenty-fifth hour in a day or an eighth day in the week, though, remains an impossible task.

Second, companies create a single pool of funding and resources for innovation. The problem with this approach is that there are big differences between types of innovation. An incremental line extension, for example, looks and feels very different from an innovation designed to create a new market. Companies that put all their innovation eggs in one basket typically find that they end up allocating all of their funds to that which is familiar and easy, leaving nothing for new growth. Create separate budgets and pools of human resources for different types of innovation.

Building Blockbuster Growth Businesses

Once you have ensured that your organization is ready for innovation, the next part of the process involves creating growth businesses. The guidance that follows describes a simple process to create what we term "new growth" businesses, or those that go beyond incremental, advancements that are similar to existing business. The principles behind the process, however, can be useful for just about any innovation effort.

At the heart of the process is the notion of disruptive innovation. As noted in chapter 1, the best path to truly transformational growth is to play the innovation game in a fundamentally different way, focusing on overlooked innovation levers like simplicity, convenience, accessibility, and affordability.

A great recent example of disruptive innovation comes from the video-gaming industry. For more than twenty years, next-generation video-game consoles competed on the basis of graphics and the complexity of the game play. Avid gamers cheered the progress that ensued. But as consoles became increasingly complicated and expensive, people who didn't have the time or the manual dexterity to furiously mash buttons found themselves left behind. In fact, the percentage of U.S. households that owned a video-game console remained flat for most of the 1990s and early 2000s.

Instead of competing on the basis of graphics quality and game-play intensity, Nintendo tried to reach non-gamers by making its Wii system intuitive and fun to play. Its controller features an accelerometer that measures motion in multiple dimensions, allowing people to control video games with arm motions instead of button mashing. Nintendo created other novel interfaces, such as its Balance Board product that allowed it to provide fitness products aimed at women. Nintendo has similarly sought to target nontraditional consumers with its handheld DS console. Games like Brain Age are designed for baby boomers. A partnership with online handbag rental company From Bags to Riches targets young women. Nintendo's strategy of making it simple and easier for more people to engage with video games has driven tremendous success. This result was no accident. Before the Wii launched in 2006, Nintendo President Satoru Iwata described Nintendo's approach: "Today there are people who play and who don't. We'll help destroy that wall between them," he said. "Regardless of age, gender or game experience, anyone can understand Wii."[2]

In industry after industry, innovators who have figured out how to drive disruption have created spectacular success stories; the three-step process that follows can help you build your own.

Step 1: Identify Opportunities

The first step of the process involves identifying opportunities for innovation. Where is the best place to look to spot opportunities? Many companies naturally look to their best, most-demanding customers. While serving those best customers is incredibly important, demanding customers don't do a good job of pointing companies toward new growth opportunities.

Instead, carefully analyze what appear to be your *worst* customers. Even better, look at customers that aren't consuming any of your products because they face some kind of *constraint on consumption*. Many great growth businesses became great by obliterating a barrier that constrained consumption. Eastman Kodak became a powerhouse because its Brownie camera expanded photography to untrained amateurs. Ryanair and easyJet became multibillion-dollar ventures by making aviation travel more affordable. Procter & Gamble created a $250 million brand in Crest Whitestrips by making teeth whitening more accessible. The Wii product made video-game playing quicker, cheaper, and more accessible (see table 4-1 for more information on identifying constraints on consumption).

TABLE 4-1

Identifying constraints on consumption

Type of constraint	Description	Examples	Analysis to identify
Skill	Expertise required to solve a problem; individuals can't do it themselves	• Photography in the late nineteenth century • Computing in the 1970s	• Map out the consumption chain of a good or service • Identify producers locked out of a market because they lack a key skill
Wealth	Current solutions are expensive, limiting consumption to the wealthy	• Airline travel prior to the 1970s • Advertising prior to the creation of cheap, simple, search advertising (à la Google's AdWords offering)	• Create a consumption pyramid • Assess whether the lower tiers of the pyramid have problems that can't be solved because solutions consumed at the top of the pyramid are too expensive
Access	Consumption can take place only in particular settings, *or* a limited variety of solutions are available	• Telephony prior to the advent of mobile phones • Movies prior to the creation of Netflix and video-on-demand offerings	• Analyze occasions when someone is unable to consume existing products • Assess whether desirable solutions are locked up and unavailable
Time	Consumption takes too long	• Buying and selling collectibles prior to the creation of eBay • Video game systems prior to the creation of the Nintendo Wii	• Assess dropouts—people who used to consume but stopped—to identify whether a lack of time influenced the decision to stop consuming • Analyze trends in required time investment to use products

Source: Scott D. Anthony, Mark W. Johnson, Joseph V. Sinfield, and Elizabeth J. Altman, *The Innovator's Guide to Growth: Putting Disruptive Innovation to Work* (Boston: Harvard Business Press, 2008).

No matter what market you select, the single most important way to pinpoint opportunities for innovation is to find out what job the target customer is struggling to get done. Remember, people don't buy products and services; they hire them to get jobs done. Look at the world through the eyes of the customer, ask what problem they can't adequately solve, and you will have the blueprint for innovation.

The jobs-to-be-done concept (introduced in the previous chapter) can immediately help you to reframe markets.[3] Milkshakes aren't simply ways to obtain calories; they provide entertainment during long boring commutes or serve as tools to appease small children. Research In Motion's popular BlackBerry device allows consumers to fill small snippets of dead time with productive activities. Companies don't really *place* advertisements in newspapers; they use advertisements as a mechanism to make their phone ring or otherwise build their business.

Remember, customers hire products to get emotional and social jobs done as well. Consider how a consumer chooses between different automobiles. While horsepower and technological features are important, the consumer considers emotional factors, such as the car's ability to provide a safe vehicle for a daily commute, and societal factors, such as the image that the car projects to neighbors and colleagues.

Really nailing the job-to-be-done is not an easy task. It typically requires blending together multiple market-research techniques and acting like an investigative reporter or detective piecing together multiple clues. Continually asking, "What important problem can't the customer solve today?" increases the chances of finding innovation opportunities.

Step 2: Formulate High-Potential Ideas

It might seem as if creating new ideas is an inherently random process. But even the most seemingly creative entrepreneurs tend to have a structured approach that helps them to develop compelling ideas. Consider the following tips:

LET PATTERNS GUIDE THE SEARCH. Innovation isn't a paint-by-number exercise. But there are clear patterns behind successful ideas. Studying disruptive developments in more than sixty different industries highlights the following key factors:

- **Start by targeting overshot customers or nonconsumers.**
  Truly disruptive change tends not to take root squarely in the mainstream of the market. Instead, disruptors tend to find a happy home among customers who don't value, and therefore don't want to pay for, the performance of high-end solutions, or those who face constraints that inhibit their ability to solve the pressing problems they face. Remember how Nintendo consciously chose to target its Wii to non-gamers.

- **Remember that good enough can be great.** Disruption is all about trade-offs, strategically lowering performance on one performance dimension to enable improvements along another dimension. Disruptors recognize that sometimes simplicity or letting customers do something themselves can be the key to success. For example, one key to Google's growth over the past few years has been the ability for customers to self-manage their advertising campaigns. A company with a high-end salesforce might consider a self-administered system inferior, but customers looking for easy and less expensive ways to manage their campaigns consider self-service to be great service.

- **Do what competitors don't want to or can't do.** Any great opportunity will inevitably encounter competition. By following an approach that looks unattractive or uninteresting to market leaders, disruptors give themselves ample room to iterate and improve their strategy. When DVD provider Netflix introduced its all-you-can-rent monthly model with no late-return penalties, traditional video-rental retailers like Blockbuster Video hesitated to respond for fear of losing profitable late fees.

USE ANALOGIES. If you find yourself struggling to come up with a good idea, step back and ask whether anyone from a different industry has tried to solve a similar problem to the one you are trying to solve. See if there is a way to apply the learning from that industry to your problem.

For example, one company was thinking about developing a disruptive strategy in the real estate market. The company's investigation led it to believe that some people felt as if they paid real estate brokers unreasonably high fees during the home-selling process. During one brainstorming session, a manager said, "What if we did for real estate what Geek Squad did for IT?" Geek Squad (part of Best Buy) provides on-demand assistance to consumers and small businesses that lack professional IT departments. The team thought about on-demand real estate assistance for people who didn't want to use real estate brokers.

By investigating similar models in the IT space, the team found that a number of companies had emerged with "reverse auction" models for IT services. In other words, a manager would go to a Web site such as Elance.com or OnForce.com and describe the problem they were facing and how much they would pay for a solution. Individual service providers would then bid for the job. The media company saw an immediate opportunity to follow a similar model in the real estate space.

If you are holding a brainstorming session, ask everyone to bring an idea from outside your industry. Ask whether you can apply the idea to the problem you are seeking to solve.

BRING TOGETHER DIVERSE GROUPS OF PEOPLE. There's a widely held view that innovation often occurs at the intersections, where people look at problems from diverse perspectives. Research by British economist John Jewkes in the 1950s confirmed this view. Jewkes found that at least forty-six of the twentieth century's fifty-eight major inventions occurred in the wrong place—in very small firms, by individuals, by people in "outgroups" in large companies, or in large companies in the wrong industry.[4] For example, a Swiss watchmaker discovered the process for the continuous casting of steel. Bringing together diverse people from within or outside your business can spur innovative ideas.

USE SIMPLE TOOLS TO CAPTURE IDEAS. Many companies unintentionally stifle innovation by creating unwieldy templates and forms for innovative ideas. Completing the
templates creates a veneer of depth, but often obfuscates the
critical issues behind success. Instead, we advocate using
simple forms, such as a one-page "Idea Résumé" that captures all of the critical elements about an idea. A simple one-
pager can enable you to tell an innovation story in a brief,
compelling way. Importantly, these kinds of tools should
highlight some of the key assumptions behind the idea, because those will be critical inputs in the next step of the
process.

Step 3: Take Ideas Forward

Many companies think that their most critical challenge is
generating more innovative ideas. Actually, that's rarely a
problem. In fact, seasoned entrepreneurs know that most
business plans aren't worth the paper on which they are
printed (or the electrons on which they are displayed). Academic research and practical experience suggest the odds that
your plan is right—particularly if you are pioneering a new
market—are infinitesimally low.[5]

Once you recognize that your first strategy is almost
always wrong, your entire approach to building business
changes. Instead of plowing huge amounts of money into a
venture, you find simple, cheap ways to test your most critical assumptions.

For example, a team in the newspaper division of the E. W.
Scripps Company had an idea to create a Web site targeting

local mothers. The team's first key assumption was that there was actually a need in its local markets. Focus groups with on-staff mothers helped to address that assumption. Then the team went on to assess whether advertisers would be interested in a mom-focused site. The Scripps team created a simple mock-up of the site and showed it to advertisers. One company tried to buy advertising on the nonexistent site on the spot—always a good sign.

Scripps then invested a little to create a market-facing pilot of the idea. As traffic and revenue grew, the company expanded to its other markets. The process of iteration didn't end though. The company continued to probe and test different business models. One idea that emerged—creating a "mom in a box" franchise that let local mothers outside of Scripps's geographies quickly open up and operate their own Web site. By following a process that constantly looked for low-cost ways to test critical assumptions, the Scripps team was able to rapidly iterate its strategy without investing huge amounts of money.

One key to making this part of the process work is to change the way you perceive failure. In many organizations, failure simply won't be tolerated. As David Kelley, the founder of famous design company IDEO, says, "Fail faster to succeed sooner." While there are clear patterns of innovation, significant risks remain. Wouldn't you rather a team fold early on, than plow hundreds of millions of dollars into a fatally flawed venture?

The next chapter provides more thoughts about how to master these kinds of "strategic experiments."

Making Innovation Repeatable

Launching a single blockbuster business is great. But success, particularly for large companies, requires launching a steady stream of blockbuster businesses. For example, think of the growth challenge facing Procter & Gamble. The consumer products titan has revenues that are fast approaching $90 billion. One of its relatively recent hits is Swiffer, a brand that within a decade reached about $900 million in revenue. That figure is astonishingly high, but it represents only 1 percent of P&G's revenues. P&G needs to create a stream of Swiffers to move its growth needle.

Making innovation systematic requires innovation *structures* and innovation *systems*.

Structuring for Success

If innovation were random, structures would inhibit success. However, because innovation can be a discipline, some kind of structure helps to spur the creation and nurturing of new growth businesses. Generally speaking, a given innovation structure can achieve one of four distinct strategic intents:

1. *Stimulate* innovation by broadening awareness and building skills. One way to achieve this strategic intent is to create training programs or internal coaches to help innovation teams ensure they are moving in the right direction. Agrichemical giant Syngenta created a customized innovation course to help intact teams use disruptive tools and approaches on specific business problems. Since forming the course in 2007,

a small team of trainers have worked with more than a dozen project teams.

2. *Shepherd* innovation by championing innovation efforts and removing obstacles that would otherwise limit the potential for innovative ideas to succeed. For example, General Electric created the Commercial Council, a team of approximately twelve of the company's senior executives. The council holds monthly conference calls and quarterly meetings to discuss, prioritize, and resource innovation proposals and growth strategies put forward by its business leaders.

3. *Spearhead* innovation by providing the resources and environment to take ideas from concept to commercialization. One approach to spearhead innovation is to create an "incubator" that works on ideas that are designed to ultimately live within the core business. Shell's GameChanger unit helps to kick-start ideas that might otherwise fall through the cracks. A second approach is to create an autonomous growth group like Cisco Systems' Emerging Technology Group, which has the mandate of creating stand-alone billion-dollar businesses. One business that came from the group is TelePresence, Cisco's high-end video-conferencing solution (discussed in chapter 9).

4. *Strengthen* innovation and enable growth by building alliances, acquiring capabilities, or

investing in innovative efforts outside the organization. For example, Intel's venture capital arm has the stated strategic intent of investing in "established and new technologies that help to develop industry standard solutions, drive global Internet growth, facilitate new usage models, and advance the computing and communications platforms."[6]

Truly world-class companies have multiple innovation structures working simultaneously. For example, at a corporate level P&G has an autonomous growth group called FutureWorks that is dedicated to "building tomorrow's brands." Within its business units, P&G has new business development groups to incubate new ideas. In 2005, P&G set up a small team of "guides" to work with project teams working on disruptive ideas. P&G's Clay Street program provides a safe place for teams to step out of day-to-day operations and explore ideas for up to three months. Senior executives manage a $100 million Corporate Innovation Fund for ideas that don't fit the normal prioritization process. Many of P&G's core brands have external advisory committees to stay abreast of key scientific developments.

This diverse array of innovation structures (many of which are described eloquently in *The Game-Changer* by P&G CEO and chairman A. G. Lafley and consultant Ram Charan) gives the company great flexibility in making sure great ideas don't fall through the cracks, while also building the organization's innovative capabilities.[7]

Systems to Support Structures

Innovation systems help to ensure that innovation structures function in appropriate ways. Again, there are myriad systems that companies can choose to implement. The following at least merit consideration:

- Market insight processes that ensure that the customer is involved in the entire innovation process. For example, Intuit, which makes Quicken, QuickBooks, and TurboTax, has a defined program by which it continually observes customers using its products to try to understand how to improve its current products and create new ones.

- Human resources policies that ensure that working on innovation is not a career killer. While financial rewards are of course important, career-path issues must be considered as well. Scripps worked carefully so that the manager who worked on its mom-focused site would not be harshly penalized if the business failed for reasons outside her control.

- Innovation-friendly measurement and tracking systems. Many companies use rigorous tools to quantify the size of an opportunity. But markets that don't exist are by definition difficult to measure and analyze. Companies need to make sure that the tools they use to measure innovation don't unintentionally show bias toward incremental, everyday innovation that is easier to measure and justify. While those innovations are important, they are not sufficient to meet most large companies' growth needs.

Summary

Growth-seeking companies have long grappled with a series of *or* statements. We can be creative *or* disciplined. We can be agile *or* reliable. We can focus on innovation *or* operational effectiveness. Success during the Great Disruption requires destroying the *or* by being creatively disciplined, reliably agile, and efficiently innovative.

The good news is that a combination of academic theory, practical guidance, and experience from world-leading companies can bring greater predictability and reliability to innovation efforts, helping companies deliver the growth they seek.

This chapter described how making innovation systematic is a three-step process:

1. Get ready for innovation by gaining control over your core, setting an innovation strategy, and allocating resources.

2. Build new growth businesses by identifying important jobs that are not being done adequately, shaping high-potential solutions, and taking ideas forward.

3. Create systems and structures to make the pursuit of growth through innovation systematic.

The innovation capabilities audit is a helpful way to bring together the first and third part of the process, ensuring the organization is ready for innovation and has the right systems and structures to make innovation repeatable (see tool 4-1). Use the diagnostic to determine your strengths and create a defined plan to tackle identified weaknesses.

TOOL 4-1

Innovation capabilities audit

Circle the box that best describes your organization's position.

Don't do it ⟶ **Do it well**

Growth blueprint

The goals (what we want) and bounds (what we won't do) for our innovation efforts are well understood.	Chaos reigns; innovation is largely random.	Generally accepted rules of thumb.	Clear view among senior leaders.	Clear view in the organization.
Our innovation portfolio is balanced.	We do not track our innovation portfolio.	Our portfolio mostly consists of close-to-the-core opportunities.	We have balance along one dimension (e.g., sectors of focus).	We have balance along multiple dimensions.
We have allocated sufficient financial and human resources to innovation.	There is no money or time for innovation.	We find people and dollars when we need them.	A small group of people have a budget for innovation.	Different groups have different budgets for innovation.

Innovation engine

We follow different approaches for different types of initiatives.	Executive judgment (or whims) guides efforts.	Core tools and metrics guide *all* innovation efforts.	Willing to "break the tools" when appropriate.	Separate tools and metrics for different types of growth initiatives.

(Continued)

We have set up appropriate organizational structures for new growth.	Demands from the core business crowd out innovation.	Personal passion can push innovation forward.	Informal structures support innovation.	Formal structures support innovation.

Supporting systems and mindsets

Senior leaders "lean forward" and help solve problems early and often.	Senior leaders are not involved in innovation.	Senior leaders review efforts at committee meetings.	Senior leaders champion specific innovation efforts.	Senior leaders are actively involved in selected efforts.
External insight is a crucial component of each stage of our process.	All innovation efforts are internally focused.	Interactions with customers in early stages of innovation process.	Interactions with customers *throughout* the process.	Ongoing interactions with customers and other external bodies.
We speak a common language of innovation.	There are discordant views of what innovation is.	A small group of managers have common views on innovation.	Codified guidelines ensure common views of innovation.	Common language is part of organizational DNA.
Staffing and incentives support our innovation strategy.	Working on innovation can have a negative impact on career.	Working on innovation has no impact on career path.	Financial rewards for people who create new innovations.	Rewards and appropriate career paths for innovators.

Number of
answers _____   _____   _____   _____

$\boxed{x}$ $\boxed{x}$ $\boxed{x}$ $\boxed{x}$

0   1   3   5

Score _____ (+) _____ (+) _____

Total Score [ ]

Implications of Score

0–5: No foundation. Have senior leaders develop a blueprint for growth.

6–20: Emerging foundation. Have small team focus on biggest weakness.

21–35: Solid foundation. Have managers develop 90-day plan to build on success.

36–45: Excellent foundation. Work with internal innovators to fine-tune approach.

5

Master Smart Strategic Experiments

In 2004, Procter & Gamble almost shut down a potentially game-changing project due to a low market forecast. The team found creative, affordable ways to test critical assumptions, and the project lived on. Companies need to find ways to remove the risk from innovation by smartly running strategic experiments.

The popular perception that innovation is risky and expensive presents challenges in uncertain economic times. That perception makes it far too easy for naysayers to justify curtailing innovation investments. After all, most of that investment isn't going to pay off anyway, right?

The constant change brought about by the Great Disruption requires companies to develop ideas more quickly and cheaply, and with lower risk. This chapter describes how the proper management of strategic experiments can help companies achieve these objectives.

The Nature of the Challenge

Many companies are very good at managing *technological* assumptions. Companies use modeling and simulation techniques, run careful experiments in laboratories, build small-scale production lines, and create physical prototypes to determine whether they can make a technology work. This carefully staged approach allows them to ensure they don't waste millions of dollars trying to commercialize a technology that just won't work.

Amazingly, companies that carefully manage these technological assumptions will fling products into the market without paying similar attention to *strategic* assumptions. And those strategic assumptions are just as important to long-term success. Is there a market need? Is the solution good enough to lead to trial? Will the customer be happy enough to repurchase, if that's required? Can you reach the customer? Will an organization's bureaucracy bog down an idea?

The principles of good experimentation are just as critical, if not more so, for strategic innovation efforts as they are for technological issues. It is very rare for an innovator to have a perfect idea from the get-go. Early discipline expedites learning that leads to critical course corrections. Conversely, companies often run into trouble when they invest tens or hundreds of millions of dollars only to learn that the strategy that looked perfect on paper flops in the market.

It is not as though companies don't *try* to confirm an idea's potential before full-scale commercialization. It's just that most techniques don't provide sufficient insight, particularly for innovations designed to create completely new markets.

For example, one way to estimate the size of a market is to gather historical data. As noted in chapter 2, the past data companies turn to suggests what *has* happened, as opposed to what *could* happen. Further, if a company has a legitimately innovative idea, what data does the researcher gather? A great example comes from IBM's exploration into the nonexistent photocopier market. In the 1950s, the company hired Arthur D. Little (ADL) to help it decide whether to purchase Xerox's patents. ADL dutifully measured the market for carbon paper, dittograph, and hectograph, and determined that capturing even 100 percent of the market at the time wouldn't justify IBM's potential investment. Of course, Xerox went on to create a multibillion-dollar market.[1] There's a reason people say markets that don't exist can't be measured and analyzed.

Another popular technique is to run concept tests. That is, show people a brief description of an idea and ask them whether they would like to purchase it. The results of these tests can feed into models that draw on historical analogues to determine an idea's potential.

This approach carries three risks. First, a consumer who *should* like an idea because it would help him or her solve an important problem might dislike a *particular* concept for myriad reasons. Maybe the concept description had words the consumer didn't like. Or the color in a picture wasn't quite right. Or the consumer simply couldn't imagine how the product or solution would fit into his or her life. The consumer's negative reaction to a concept obscures the fact that the company is working in the right market space. Statisticians would call this kind of "false negative" a Type II error. For example, Procter & Gamble's Swiffer product showed sufficiently low scores in its concept test that the company considered killing the product, which, of course, went on to become a blockbuster success.

Second, consumers might also react positively to a concept because they find it novel, but when it comes to actual purchase, they realize that the problem the product addresses isn't important enough to part with their hard-earned cash. Statisticians would call this a Type I error; we call it a Pet Rock problem after a line of products from the mid-1970s that had six months of popularity before becoming a historical footnote.

Finally, models that draw on historical analogues rely on comparing the results of a concept test to similar products or services. This approach works well when the comparison set is clear. For example, a line extension for Tide can draw on dozens of clearly parallel examples in the laundry aisle of the supermarket. But what is the right comparison for a category-creating product?

For example, in 2004 P&G faced a critical decision about a project to introduce a probiotic solution to treat the symptoms of irritable bowel syndrome (IBS). While IBS is a common condition—estimates suggest that at least 30 million people in the United States alone suffer from IBS—many sufferers don't even know they have IBS. They just know they can't eat certain foods, have to be near a restroom when they go to the movies, and should avoid activities where there are no toilets, such as boat rides.

P&G was on the verge of killing the idea. Despite clinical evidence that the product—now in the market under the brand name Align—worked, and despite positive response from consumers who tried the product, the projected market seemed small, especially given looming expenditures related to improving the product's shelf stability so that Align could safely reside in P&G's traditional retail sales channel.

One challenge facing the deal was determining the right comparison for Align. Was it like vitamin supplements that come in pill form? Some other supplement? Or was it Prilosec, a treatment for symptoms of heartburn that requires daily use? The lack of an obvious comparison made it difficult to accurately forecast the product's sales.

A final challenge related to drawing on historical analogues is the fact that most disruptive success stories involve course correction on the path to success. A comparison that looks appropriate in the concept phase can be 180 degrees off as the strategy shifts.

A Different Approach

Relying on past data or customer response to a proposal on paper is inadequate. Fortunately, innovators can draw on research by Howard Mintzberg, Robert Burgelman, Rita McGrath, Clayton Christensen, and others to improve their ability to manage strategic experiments.[2] Following the approach discussed next—focusing on key assumptions and finding simple and cheap ways to test those assumptions—can also substantially improve the productivity of idea development efforts.

The first step is to pinpoint the most critical assumptions behind success.[3] The best way to identify critical assumptions is to pick up an idea and look at it from multiple perspectives. Think about what would have to go right strategically for an idea to succeed. A simple way to do this is to tell a story of what the business looks like at steady state. Start by evaluating how consumers experience the business. What are they buying? Why are they buying it? How do they find out about it? How do they pay for it? Then, talk about how the *company* experiences the business. What is it doing? How is it doing it? How does money flow? Why is leadership excited? Then look through the lens of the channel, partners, and key suppliers. What are they doing to support the business? Why are they excited to do what they are doing? Telling this kind of story can help to identify whether there is a weak link in the business, such as consumers never hearing about the idea, the company squashing the idea, or a key partner not helping to support the idea.

While each innovation is different, companies should watch for four common strategic traps that might appear in their story:

1. **No customer job-to-be-done.** The best innovations help customers solve a pressing problem. Companies can sometimes fall in love with an idea without truly understanding whether the customer is similarly in love with it.

2. **Underestimation of competitive response.** Clayton Christensen's research on disruptive innovation shows that market leaders almost always win when the battle is about bringing better products and services to existing markets (in Christensen's language, "sustaining" innovations). Powerful companies that try to edge into new markets can underestimate how fiercely the market leader will defend its turf.

3. **The sucking sound of the core.** A company's core business is a powerful magnet. It can take the most interesting idea and slowly, subtly reshape it so it resembles what the company has done in the past, rather than something truly novel. After all, you *can* fit a square peg in a round hole if you make the peg small enough. Unless managed carefully, internal stakeholders can squash or shrink potentially novel ideas.

4. **Channel misalignment.** People don't do what doesn't make sense to them. When a company asks a sales channel to prioritize something that promises to make less money than other alternatives, it should not be surprised when the channel balks.

Next, think about the financial aspect. Instead of creating a spreadsheet several tabs deep, build a "three *p*" market-sizing calculation. What is the addressable *population*? Is there any analogue product or service that might show what kind of *penetration* might be possible? What *price* points are possible? This kind of simple calculation can help identify critical assumptions behind success (see "Financials and Disruptive Innovation" for more).

Generating assumptions shouldn't be a solitary exercise. Seek to involve as many perspectives as possible, because people with topical expertise might see a risk that appears invisible to nonexperts.

The next step is to identify the most critical assumptions. Generally speaking, a critical assumption has one or more of the following characteristics:

- Deal killers—an assumption proving false would derail the entire business. For example, if you are assuming that customers will pay for a product and they won't, the odds that you will be able to create a successful strategy are very low.

- Path dependencies—addressing a critical assumption unlocks other assumptions. Imagine you are walking down a path, and you decide to take a fork that leads to a river. Once you get to the river you find it is frozen. You could not have known that the river was frozen if you hadn't first decided to follow the fork in the path. Assumptions about channel choices can have high path dependencies because they influence other aspects of the strategy.

- Importance to investors or stakeholders who ultimately make decisions about innovations.

- Uncertain areas that have significant impact on an idea's ultimate potential.

FINANCIALS AND DISRUPTIVE INNOVATION

In an interview with Innosight in 2007, Intuit founder and chairman Scott Cook expressed his view of the utility of detailed financial forecasts for disruptive initiatives.

> We tell our disruptive teams to not do volume forecasts. Do not do a spreadsheet with volume forecasts on it, because it is unforecastable. You really cannot know. So why waste the time doing bogus numbers that are unknowable. The finance department may ask for them, so spend five minutes, do something quickly, but the leadership should not focus on those numbers. They are wrong, you just don't know in what direction. Instead we have teams focus on how deep is the customer problem that's unserved and how good is our solution at solving it. If those two are strong, then we have a reasonable shot at a good business. If either of those is weak, then no matter what the spreadsheet says, no matter what the volume forecast says, there is not a business here.

We generally agree with Cook. Trying to piece together financials can be a useful way to identify critical assumptions, or to ensure that a business passes a basic "sniff test." Using the results of assumptions layered upon assumptions to make decisions is silly.

It is vital to focus on the short list of critical areas to address at any one time. A team will have dozens, if not hundreds, of assumptions. But it is impossible to test hundreds of things simultaneously, particularly when resources are scarce. Our experience suggests that in a given time period, a team should be thinking about no more than three primary assumptions and three secondary assumptions. The discipline from identifying this short list helps to ensure proper focus in the next part of the process.

Testing Critical Assumptions

P&G chairman and CEO A. G. Lafley is a strong believer in moving beyond traditional concept tests to more transaction-oriented learning, where people in essence "vote with their wallet." In a May 2008 discussion, Lafley noted that transaction-based learning

> is really important because it's when you begin to understand who the prospect really is for this new product or service, will they purchase it and for how much, and then, once they purchase it, what's the usage cycle like, what prompts repurchase?
>
> In my world consumers cannot really tell us what they want. If we exposed something to them as a stimulus, they can say, "I like it," or "I don't like it," and they can tell you why they like it or why they don't like it, but they cannot tell you what they want. Nobody told us that they wanted Crest Whitestrips; nobody told us that they were dying for a Swiffer; nobody told

us that Febreze would make their life better. So, consumers cannot tell us what they want . . . I've become a pretty big believer in getting that idea or technology to some relatively clear concept expression and some relatively crude prototype as fast as you possibly can, and then get that in front of prospective consumers or customers.[4]

As P&G has worked to develop a competency in disruptive innovation over the past few years, it has focused on finding ways to test key assumptions in the market. For example, in early 2008, it distributed a potentially game-changing diaper to a handful of consumers at a local amusement park. It then began selling the product over the Internet. These low-visibility efforts helped the team learn what kind of parents would seek out the product. Interacting closely with Internet purchasers and watching chatter in the blogosphere allowed the company to learn a great deal about how parents viewed the product.

Another disruptive initiative is Swash, a line of fabric-care products targeting the 30 percent of garments that are re-worn without being laundered. P&G had natural questions about whether the target consumer was a college student or a time-starved mother. So it opened a small store in Ohio and started selling Swash over the Internet. It found that the proposition appealed to both consumer groups for differ ent reasons, of course.

A final example is Align, the probiotic discussed earlier. In 2004, Innosight helped the Align team reframe its approach.

Instead of trying to come up with a definitive answer about Align's potential, the team identified what would have to be true to create a business about which P&G could get excited. The team zeroed in on the critical assumptions it would have to test to believe in the idea's potential. Would doctors promote Align? Would consumers who had to take a pill every day for three weeks before they saw results and keep taking the pill to stop symptoms from reappearing actually comply with the daily regimen?

P&G decided to learn about these assumptions without making the product shelf stable enough to sell in mass-market retailers. The team quietly offered the product on the Internet. It didn't invest tens of millions of dollars on advertising. Rather, its existing pharmaceutical salesforce promoted the product to doctors in three cities. Internet-based sales facilitated P&G's ability to learn whether consumers were trying, repeating, and repurchasing.

Important insights came from this process. Instead of simply having a vial with a bunch of pills in it, the Align team created a blister pack with days of the week to remind consumers to take the pill every day. Branding changed as well. Initial packaging said Align was "from the makers of Metamucil." P&G dropped Metamucil and let Align stand alone.

As the team began expanding to work with more doctors in more cities, some of P&G's traditional retail customers like Walgreens began offering the product online. In 2007, the team started using a pharmacy distribution channel, which meant any pharmacy in the United States could call a wholesaler and receive the product within twenty-four hours. It continued to sell the product directly online. In 2008, it made the product available to traditional retailers in three cities. In early 2009, the product launched nationally. "The team stair-stepped to market, never investing ahead of learning," P&G Chief Technology Officer Bruce Brown noted. "It is very consistent with the disruptive pattern."[5]

Of course, there are other strategic experiments (the appendix highlights strategic experiments from *The Innovator's Guide to Growth*) in addition to running transaction tests. The simplest experiment involves picking up the phone and talking to industry experts, venture capitalists, or prospective customers to pick their brains about the idea.

Companies can also run focused experiments on key assumptions. For example, Turner Broadcasting had a novel advertising idea for its television networks. Inspired by the success of online and print contextual advertisement placement, a team at Turner wondered if it could introduce a similar idea on television. Imagine a scene in a television show that ends with a child covered in mud, followed immediately with an advertisement for laundry detergent. Academic research indicated that this kind of contextual linkage made an advertisement more memorable. Turner was in a unique position to commercialize this idea, as networks like TNT and TBS present hundreds of movies and popular television series, such as *Law & Order* and *Seinfeld,* next to advertising units that could be strategically placed.

Building the systems to do contextual advertising at sufficient scale looked expensive. Before making the investment, Turner wanted to make sure that its programs had enough scenes that would be of interest to traditional television advertisers. By having interns tag a handful of programs, it quickly learned that their movies and shows did have meaningful moments of context, and that those contextual moments would appeal to leading advertisers. Turner decided to move the idea forward. Its system, called TVinContext, debuted in early 2008.

Keys to Success

Successfully managing strategic experiments requires a delicate balance. Experimentation is critical, but not without risk. Experiments can take time and can be expensive. They can perpetuate, which may lead a company to miss an opportunity while continuing to experiment (see "The Hidden Value of Fast Kills"). And they can expose an idea to the market prematurely.

The following tips can help companies maximize returns on investments in learning.

FOCUS CAREFULLY ON THE METRICS THAT DETERMINE WHETHER AN EXPERIMENT IS A SUCCESS OR FAILURE. Companies should carefully predict the results of an experiment—even if the actual answer is completely unknown and unknowable. Steven Spear's excellent book *Chasing the Rabbit* describes how the navy followed this approach in the early days of a program to create nuclear-powered submarines. The head of the project asked scientists to predict how neutron bombardments would fatigue the metal that shielded the reactor. No one really knew what the results would be. But making

THE HIDDEN VALUE OF FAST KILLS

One of the hardest decisions companies face is when to put a project on ice. After all, companies don't start an effort without a belief in an ultimate payoff. And even ideas that struggle to gain traction present compelling "what if" scenarios.

"Fast kills," where a company pulls the plug on a doomed effort early, have three advantages:

1. **Cost savings.** Commercializing projects takes money. If companies can identify flawed ideas early, they can avoid having to make investments that won't pay out.

2. **Increased throughput.** The time a customer spends waiting in a supermarket queue is a function of the number of customers, the speed of each transaction, and the number of open registers. Projects can sit in the corporate equivalent of a supermarket checkout line, with the number of project contributors, the scarcity of executive bandwidth, and so on having an impact on the throughput. Lowering the number of projects can dramatically increase the speed of the remaining projects.

3. **Improved output.** Companies that shut down bad projects early can reallocate talented managers to the remaining ideas. This kind of "doubling down" can make the good projects even better.

(Continued)

Data-minded companies can roughly quantify these benefits. For example, calculating the average investment and success rate for similar projects can provide an estimate of potential cost savings. Using a concept called "Little's Law" can help to estimate the increase in throughput by running fewer projects through a system. Determining the impact of a greater probability of realizing positive scenarios can provide a ballpark estimate of the value of focusing more deeply on fewer ideas.

When companies decide to shutter efforts early, they should make sure they capture key learning from the effort and publicly laud the no-longer-in-existence team. Not every idea is destined for greatness. Teams that learn this early have helped to advance the company's overall innovation efforts.

predictions, designing sensors to check the predictions, and carefully evaluating the results helped scientists develop a much deeper understanding about the process. This kind of approach has helped the naval program experience an astonishingly low rate of accidents during its fifty-year tenure.[6]

Spear notes that this focus on measuring, learning, and adjusting is common in "high velocity organizations" that constantly outpace their competitors. "By making abundantly clear what is expected to occur, it is much easier to be surprised by the things that happen which have not been anticipated," Spear writes. "Clear expectations don't, in themselves, make things go right. Clear expectations simply make it obvious when things do not go as expected. So it is easier to say, 'Oh, that's not what I thought would happen. There is something about this process I don't understand and need to learn.'"[7]

Companies that use this approach to manage strategic assumptions will similarly find that careful consideration of the results of an experiment before (and after) it is run can help to expedite rapid testing and adjustment. Without this careful process, companies can miss important strategic insights.

In 2006, a newspaper company ran a six-week test of a new online advertising offering. We held a meeting to discuss the test's results. "The idea was a bomb," said the manager who oversaw the pilot. "Why?" I asked. "We only recorded $500 in revenue in six weeks!" he responded. That certainly didn't sound good, but I decided to probe a bit more deeply. "How many sales did that represent?" I asked. "Four," the manager responded. No hope yet. "How many salespeople were involved in the trial?" "Ten." Still sounds reasonable. "How many businesses did the ten salespeople approach?" The manager rifled through his notes. "Seven," he responded. Aha!

We had stumbled on an important insight. In fact, the offering connected quite closely with the target customer—four of seven customers approached by the company purchased the product, a rate that exceeded expectations. The problem was that the salesforce wasn't particularly interested in pushing the product, even after extensive training with senior leaders. Most salespeople viewed the idea as a costly distraction. The price point was low, so commissions would be low too. Salespeople had to call on customers they didn't usually serve, which they perceived to be a low-return effort. Better understanding of the key variables behind success would have helped the company do a better job managing the experiment and increased the odds of developing a successful business.

USE THE SCARCITY PRINCIPLE TO LOWER THE COST OF EXPERIMENTATION. One of the mantras of the disruptive innovator is "patient for growth, impatient for profits." Companies that follow this approach test their critical assumptions quickly and avoid overdesigning offerings with features that aren't meaningful to end customers.

It has never been easier to test an idea quickly and cheaply. Recall the examples in chapter 1: $15,000 in 2007 for Guy Kawasaki to launch his business, and $500 by Jessica Mah in 2008 to launch an internship job board. The ability to use the Internet, low-cost specialists, and modeling and simulation tools make it easy for companies to innovate on the cheap.

There are many ways to embrace the scarcity principle. Instead of building a physical prototype, use a three-dimensional illustration. Run quick-and-dirty market research using tools such as SurveyMonkey.com. Have consumers request samples via a Web site instead of through in-store trials. Tap into prediction markets to develop rough market forecasts. Use friends, families, and coworkers as sources of inspiration for ideas.

LIMIT THE TIME FOR AN EXPERIMENT. Companies that don't make decisions rapidly can find that their innovation process slows to a crawl as experiments perpetuate. Coupling the scarcity principle with quick decision making can paradoxically make innovation faster, cheaper, and more successful.

THINK CAREFULLY ABOUT ISOLATED (FOCUSED ON ONE ELEMENT) VERSUS INTEGRATED (END-TO-END) EXPERIMENTS. Testing too many things at once can make it hard to tease out whether an experiment proved or disproved a hypothesis. On the other hand, some assumptions can be tested only using more integrated approaches such as test markets.

MONITOR YOUR PROJECT'S BURN RATE. One ten-person project team spent three months debating whether to run a $500,000 test. The fully loaded cost of the team per month was about $175,000, meaning the cost of deciding whether to run the test ($525,000) was more than the test itself. Teams within large companies often forget that even when they are not spending money, *they are spending money*. Understanding burn rates at a detailed level can be critical to help manage the strategic experimentation process. Of course, good entrepreneurs generally seek to minimize fixed costs as much as possible. Using contractors or having other flexible arrangements can help to keep costs under control (the next chapter has more about sharing innovation risks).

REMEMBER TO SAVOR SURPRISES. One company used its technological acumen to earn a commanding lead in a category. Its competitor launched a product that intentionally traded off pure performance to provide much greater convenience to the customer. The market leader conducted research that discovered customers preferred the competitor's product. The market leader's first reaction? The survey must be wrong. There was no way the customer could prefer a lower-performing product. The company took more than two years to respond, not because of the technical sophistication of the competitor's product, but because it didn't "savor," or embrace and explore the implications of, the surprising news that it discovered.

EXPECT AND TOLERATE FAILURE. While General Motors has had its share of problems over the past few years, one shining success is its OnStar telematics business. The company's first strategy—OnStar as a completely separate business sold as a postsales add-on—was problematic. Consumers didn't understand OnStar's benefit, and dealers struggled to push the product. So GM decided to install OnStar as a standard option on many of its cars and give customers free service for a year so they could experience the system's benefit. While OnStar has a separate internal board of directors and is run fairly independently, integration with the car business turned out to be crucial. Costs are lower and margins are higher by making the technology factory-standard, and because the unit is in all GM cars, many more customers end up subscribing to the monthly service.

In 2007 as the business crossed $1 billion in revenue, CEO Rick Wagoner reflected on the lessons he learned. "With a new business you may start out with a strategy, but after about four days you probably change it, and that has been very much the way OnStar's played out for us," Wagoner said. "It's been fascinating to see how it's developed, and it has changed how I think about opportunities in the rest of our business. You don't have to figure it out a hundred percent. If you think it is right, get on the road and adjust as you go."[8]

REMEMBER THAT PEOPLE, NOT TOOLS, MAKE DECISIONS ABOUT INNOVATION PROJECTS. Innovation still requires intuition and judgment. Making decisions based purely on the numbers can be a strategic mistake.

"If you use the spreadsheets to try to discriminate and predict which businesses will succeed and fail you'll be utterly off," Intuit Founder and Chairman Scott Cook says. "Because the failures had just as pretty spreadsheets as the successes."[9] Instead, Cook and his team push project teams to test ideas in the marketplace in four weeks. The short time frame forces teams to focus on critical assumptions and design "good enough" solutions.

For example, one team was working on an idea that would be a matching service between accountants who had too much work at a given time and accountants who had some extra capacity. According to Cook, "I said, 'That's a nice theory but this won't work unless you have both demand from accountants with too much work and supply from accountants who are good but for some reason are sitting on their hands.'" In three weeks, the team built a functional prototype and did a mailing to about fifty thousand accountants to test demand. They learned that there were indeed competent accountants who had excess capacity, supporting further investment in the idea.

Summary

Often, the reason that people perceive innovation to be risky and expensive is their failure to couple technical experimentation with strategic experimentation. The right strategic experiments can help companies improve the productivity of their learning efforts. To master strategic experimentation, remember to:

- Focus on the most critical risks—potential deal killers, path-dependent elements, items that matter to stakeholders, and so on

- Design smart, cheap ways to learn about those risks, with a bias toward market-based learning

- Balance the need to experiment with some of the risks of experimentation

- Embrace the scarcity principle

- Savor surprises

6

Share the Innovation Load

Robert Reiss cleared a cool $2 million in 1984 by assembling
a network of partners to opportunistically attack an opportunity
in the board-game market. Companies don't have to go it
alone. Sharing the load can make innovation more
manageable—and more successful.

Smart strategic experiments can lower innovation expenses
and risk. Another way to achieve those outcomes is to share
the innovation burden with other parties, spreading investment and risk to customers, suppliers, and even competitors
that are best positioned to bear it.

The benefits of sharing the innovation load aren't unique
to tough economic times. It is almost always a good thing to
partner with people who are more capable of or specialized
in solving particular problems. Once again, belt tightening

can force innovators to follow practices that they should have been following already.

The Entrepreneur's Instinct

Many entrepreneurs find smart risk sharing to be highly intuitive. For example, one of the Harvard Business School's best-selling cases is an interesting study from the early 1980s about entrepreneur Robert Reiss.[1] Reiss made a few million dollars pouncing on an opportunity to create a trivia game just as that category was nearing its peak.

As Trivial Pursuit began to take off in Canada in 1984, Reiss's industry experience told him there was a short-term window of opportunity in the United States. He wrote a letter to TV Guide to see if the company would partner with him to promote a trivia game and to write TV-based trivia questions. He entered into an agreement with one of his friends to design the game. Swiss Colony, a catalog company, agreed to handle warehousing and distribution. Reiss paid a third party to expedite collections from slow-paying retailers.

He went from the nugget of an idea to a fully fledged board-game business in less than a year. All in all, Reiss invested about $50,000 of his own capital. He personally made more than $2.1 million (more than $4 million in today's dollars) within twelve months. That's a tidy 4,100 percent return. Reiss's partners were all richly rewarded for their efforts.

The beauty of Reiss's model is that he found the best people to handle each element of the business. The teaching point: good entrepreneurs don't *take* risk, they *manage* risk. Starting a new venture is risky enough as it is. Not only is trying to develop capabilities in areas where expertise is accessible and affordable unnecessary, it increases the chances of failure.

Five Angles to Explore

Entrepreneurs have a risk-sharing mentality because they simply have no other choice. Fortunately, the notion of smart risk sharing has seeped into the corporate world over the past decade. Henry Chesbrough from the University of California Berkeley captured the trend eloquently in his 2003 book *Open Innovation*.[2] Building on work by academics such as Eric von Hippel from the Massachusetts Institute of Technology, Chesbrough argued that companies could no longer rely on centralized, closed research and development efforts. Instead, they had to connect to external innovators to identify ideas, solve problems, and build businesses.

Procter & Gamble recognized the power of open innovation early on. The company set—and subsequently exceeded—a lofty goal that more than 50 percent of innovations would feature some kind of outside involvement by the end of the decade. P&G's effort, Connect + Develop, sought to shift its attitude "from resistance to innovations 'not invented here' to enthusiasm for those 'proudly found elsewhere.'"[3]

Companies should explore at least five specific risk-sharing angles: customers, external experts, channel partners, competitors, and start-up companies. Considering these and other options to spread the innovation burden will allow companies to innovate faster, better, and cheaper.

Customers

A core premise of Chesbrough's work is that customers who are close to particular problems can be better at dreaming up solutions to the problems than companies themselves. For example, one of Innosight's colleagues recently did work for a leading medical device company. He asked the company to state the origin of the twenty most exciting ideas in one particular product category. It turned out that many game-changing medical devices originated not from multibillion dollar companies, but from individual physicians or small start-up companies.[4]

Why were the individuals able to do what the medical device company couldn't do? It turned out that developing a new idea didn't require millions of dollars of investment. It required a doctor who understood a problem, a mechanical engineer to develop a solution, and about $25,000.

Scaling that innovation was another matter entirely. But the industry fit the three basic requirements that allow for distributed innovation:

1. **Well-defined problems.** If a problem can't be adequately defined, the chances are low that an individual can design a viable solution.

2. **Self-contained problems.** If a successful solution needs to interact seamlessly with other organizational

processes or designs, it is difficult for an outsider without deep inside knowledge to adequately solve the problem. For example, when Intel designs a new microprocessor, it needs close coordination between its design team and its manufacturing team. A solution created by an outsider wouldn't be "plug compatible."

3. **Small-scale solutions.** Individual investors typically have limited budgets. If developing a solution costs hundreds of millions of dollars, individual inventors simply can't create meaningful solutions. After all, how could an entrepreneur in a garage spend hundreds of millions of dollars creating a next-generation microprocessor?

Companies like Kraft, Dell, and Starbucks have demonstrated the power of customer-driven innovation. For example, several years ago, Gary Schwartzberg had an idea to create a tube-shaped bagel packed with cream cheese.[5] Riding on the wave of convenience products, Schwartzberg envisioned a blockbuster product that would appeal to time-starved consumers. He patented a method for inserting the cream cheese into the bagel so that it stayed intact during baking.

He tried to commercialize the product himself and learned that getting national distribution can be a difficult task for an individual entrepreneur. So he brought his idea to Kraft. The food giant formed an alliance with Schwartzberg, rebranded the product as "Bagel-Fuls," inserted its Philadelphia brand cream cheese in the bagels, and got national distribution almost overnight. This was part of a conscious effort by Kraft to tap into the broader market for ideas. Its idea-sharing Web site, www.innovatewithkraft.com, gathers an average of fifty new ideas each month.

Companies can also enlist customers to play an active role in shaping or creating products. Google's search algorithm relies on looking at how Web sites link to other Web sites. Amazon.com has millions of user-submitted product reviews. Wikipedia's fully community-dependent model has become a vital hub for researchers.[6]

Users can be actively involved in businesses that involve physical products as well. Threadless.com features user-submitted T-shirt designs that they vote on. The company only produces T-shirts that have sufficient demand, allowing it to minimize costly inventory.

External Experts

Historically, companies derived competitive advantage from excellence in research and development or invention. Bring enough creative scientists or marketers together, and they can crack tough problems or dream up the next big thing.

However, as problems get tougher and knowledge becomes more diffuse, companies are finding it progressively more difficult to monopolize talent. Instead, they are finding ways to tap into focused problem solvers, wherever they may reside.

For example, InnoCentive Open Innovation Marketplace— a spin-off of pharmaceutical giant Eli Lilly—makes a market between companies trying to solve tough research problems and individual scientists. Companies describe their specific problem online and spell out what constitutes a successful solution. As an example, the Oil Spill Recovery Institute of Cordova, Alaska, was looking for a way to keep oil from freezing in frigid Alaskan storage tanks. It was willing to pay $20,000 to an individual or group of scientists that could detail how they would solve the problem. A chemist based in Illinois had discovered that vibrating concrete kept it from setting before it was poured. Applying that discovery to the Alaskan oil challenge netted the chemist the prize (with InnoCentive receiving a portion). As of 2008, InnoCentive had successfully hosted hundreds of searches.[7]

There are other specialist providers that target big companies, such as YourEncore, which helps companies find retired workers who have specialized skills and are seeking part-time work; NineSigma, which matches companies and inventors with patents; and ProfessionaLink, which is a kind of headhunter for consulting companies. Emerging models like Elance.com, Guru.com, and GetAFreelancer.com make it significantly easier and cheaper for smaller companies to tap into individual experts. One estimate suggested that these kinds of marketplaces facilitated close to $2 billion in transactions in 2008.[8]

A final way to locate individual experts is to run innovation contests. For example, in 1996 the X Prize Foundation offered $10 million for the first successful private space flight. In 2007, Netflix announced it would provide substantial rewards to anyone who could improve the accuracy of its recommendation algorithm by 10 percent. The basic concept is that expertise can be anywhere, so companies need to thoughtfully find ways to attract and motivate talent.

Channel and Other Partners

It is rare for a company to control an entire production system itself. Almost every company has suppliers, partners, and a channel to reach end-consumers. These value chain participants can be key innovation partners as well.

Retailers have a rich history of innovating with suppliers. For example, Target has developed an approach to democratize high-end designs to fit the company's "cheap chic" approach. Five years ago, it started working with individual designers like Isaac Mizrahi to create attractive products that could be manufactured and sold at reasonable prices.

Revlon became an almost accidental example of intelligent risk sharing when it introduced opaque nail polish in the 1930s. At the time, most polishes were colored with dyes and came in three shades of red. Revlon's polish was made with pigment, which made it last longer and opened the possibility of an expanded range of shades and colors. Like many companies in the 1930s, Revlon had difficulty obtaining bank financing, so it had to rely on loan sharks. As Charles Revson, who cofounded the company with his brother Joseph and chemist Charles Lachman, said, "The first year or so we gave the Shylocks plenty of business—we used to pay two percent a month to stay alive." Revson borrowed space from relatives and had his mother work for the business until she died of an infection in 1933.[9]

The lack of solid funding inhibited Revlon's ability to launch a broad marketing campaign and sell its product in mass-market retailers. Instead, Charles Revson noted that beauty salons and manicures were booming in popularity. Revlon started selling its product to wholesalers who targeted salons. The lower-risk approach had a side benefit of creating opportunities for executives to get close to the consumers. In its first nine months of operation in 1932, the company rang up more than $4,000 in sales. In 1934, it received a substantial order from Marshall Field's. Sales multiplied more than forty times by 1937, and the company was on its way to success.

Innovating with suppliers or channel partners requires remembering one overriding principle: people do not do what doesn't make sense to them. The double negative in that sentence is important. Companies get into trouble when they ask a sales channel to prioritize an opportunity that promises to make the channel less money than other opportunities, or when they ask a supplier to do something that would decimate its business.

Consider how long it has taken digital film projectors to enter the mainstream. Pioneering director George Lucas predicted that by the time the third episode of his *Star Wars* prequel was ready, thousands of movie theaters would be using digital projectors. But when the movie launched in 2005, only one hundred of more than thirty-six thousand movie screens in the United States used digital technologies.

While movie *makers* preferred the flexibility of digital technologies and movie *studios* preferred their low cost, the economics just didn't make sense for movie *theaters*. Operators had to pay upward of $100,000 for projectors that didn't provide any near-term revenue boosts. Only recently have digital technologies taken off as prices have dropped and theaters have experimented with new revenue-generating approaches, such as piping in live sporting events or concerts.[10]

Competitors

It might seem heretical to think about collaborating with a competitor. However, working closely with competitors can allow companies to realize new growth. Generally, this kind of arrangement works best when one company has an enabling technology that fits with a competitor's brand or sales channel.

For example, P&G and The Clorox Company are fierce competitors in the laundry aisle, but P&G has no brands that compete with Clorox's Glad product line. In the early 2000s, P&G developed technology that had applicability in that business. Without the right manufacturing facilities or brands, P&G would need to invest tens of millions of dollars to enter into a bruising battle with an entrenched competitor. Instead, P&G decided to partner with Clorox to commercialize the technology. The Press'n Seal food wrap and Force-Flex garbage bags that resulted from the partnership created substantial growth—for both companies. These kinds of efforts require deep understanding about corporate strengths and weaknesses, but can be a way to realize growth that otherwise would be inaccessible.

Companies can also consider partnering with competitors to share costs. For example, a number of newspaper companies have "joint operating agreements" in which they share printing plants and other fixed costs in local markets. In late 2008, some local television stations followed suit by announcing plans to pool high-cost news-gathering resources like helicopters. Sharing costs with competitors makes sense when a particular cost is required but doesn't drive competitive advantage.

Start-up Companies

Finally, companies can tap into start-up companies for the development of new technologies, products, or even capabilities.

Companies have long looked to acquire start-up companies to plug gaps in their development road maps. The companies that do this best approach the problem in a systematic way. Between 1993 and 2006, for example, Cisco Systems made more than one hundred acquisitions, roughly one every six weeks for thirteen years. During that time, Cisco's dedicated team of acquisition specialists developed a structured approach to ensure it maximized the return from its investment in new companies. Specifically, the team mapped out rules to increase the odds that an acquisition would succeed and created a step-by-step process to integrate acquired companies.[11]

Companies often think about acquiring people, technology, or brands, but sometimes the most valuable asset in an acquisition is a capability or a channel. Examples include Cisco's acquisition of Linksys and WebEx, CVS Caremark's acquisition of MinuteClinic, Best Buy's acquisition of Geek Squad, and News Corporation's acquisition of MySpace parent Intermix Media, Inc. In each case, the acquirer got accumulated knowledge about working with different channels, targeting different customers, and making money in different ways. Innovation-seeking companies should always be on the lookout for how they can use acquisitions to build capabilities that can be extended into new markets.

Companies can do more than acquire start-ups. They also can make small investments in or form strategic alliances with start-up companies. These kinds of approaches allow a company to learn more about an emerging market space or technology without making big investments. Even in today's frigid venture climate, toeing into new waters can help companies spot new ideas and strategies early and help spur companies that might ultimately demand the company's core product. Intel has successfully followed this strategy. Its Intel Capital venture arm has created substantial financial returns while seeding businesses that create new demand for Intel's microprocessors.

Summary

Entrepreneurs don't take risk, they manage risk. The best entrepreneurs expertly find people who are the best in the world at a particular task and find productive ways to work together to achieve common goals. Companies looking to do more with less need to borrow this entrepreneurial mind-set and smartly share risk with customers, external experts, channel partners, competitors, and start-up companies. Using these and other innovation partners can help companies lower the costs and the risks of innovation.

7

Learn to Love the Low End

In the dark days of October 2008, consumers flocked to
discounters like Wal-Mart and McDonald's. Increasingly value-
conscious customers and hungry low-cost competitors mean
that innovators have to learn how to love the low end. Slashing
prices isn't enough. Determine what customers in low-end
segments value . . . and deliver it.

The previous chapters described what companies are currently doing that they need to *stop,* and what they are currently doing that they need to do *differently.* This chapter and the next describe what most companies are not doing that they need to *start.*

In uncertain times, companies need to love the low end by embracing low-cost approaches that appeal to increasingly value-conscious customers and serve as a vital defense mechanism against encroaching attackers.

In 1999, such a low-cost attacker appeared on General Electric's radar screen. The company, SonoSite, had created a handheld portable ultrasound device called iLook. The device was much simpler and cheaper than GE's traditional ultrasound devices. In classic disruptive fashion, it took root, not in the mainstream market, but among personal care physicians who were interested in using ultrasound on patients they normally would refer to specialists.

Typically, market-leading incumbents ignore these kinds of developments, giving the disruptor space to hone their offering. Then, the disruptor begins to pick off pieces of the business that the incumbent cares about. When it becomes clear that response is critical, it is too late. Companies like Southwest Airlines, Wal-Mart, Infosys, Dell Computer, and Charles Schwab used this kind of disruptive approach to transform markets and cause leaders to topple.

GE, however, did something different. In 2002, it introduced a handheld version of its Logiq line of products to compete directly with SonoSite's iLook line. By 2006, GE had become the world leader in portable ultrasounds, with annual sales of close to $200 million.

Historically, GE's successful mastery of what the literature calls a "low-end" approach would be a screaming anomaly to the finding that entrants almost always triumph in battles of disruptive innovation. But incumbent companies like Dow Corning, Cisco, ING, Intel, and Teradyne have demonstrated that low-end strategies are within the grasp of well-run market leaders (see "Incumbents That Have Launched Low-end Businesses" at the end of the chapter). Studying the pattern of low-end attackers and the successes— and struggles—of market leaders suggests a very clear, four-step approach to loving the low end. Companies that spot low-end opportunities, shape low-cost solutions, build viable low-end business models, and create appropriate organizational structures will dramatically increase their chances of deflecting disruptive threats and seizing previously unattainable growth opportunities.

Step 1: Spot Low-end Opportunities

Typically, low-end businesses first target customers who are "overshot" by existing products and services. That begs two questions. First, what precisely is overshooting? Second, what are the signs that overshooting has set in? In short, overshooting means that companies provide more performance along a particular dimension than a given group of customers really cares about or can afford. Those customers will always *take* a product or service that outstrips their needs; they just don't want to pay for features that they don't care about.

Companies overshoot a market by doing what they are supposed to do—making existing products better so they can raise prices. At some point, this process results in customers receiving diminishing marginal benefit from improvements that used to matter to them. The net effect is they stop paying price premiums for these improvements and are ready to switch to lower-price solutions.

While precisely identifying overshooting can be difficult, four gut-check questions can help a company see whether overshooting has begun.[1]

1. **Are people hesitating to update to new products?** The general ambivalence many users have about upgrading to Microsoft's latest operating system (Vista) or to its Office 2007 product suite indicates that people are generally satisfied with the features and functionality of existing products.

2. **Are low-cost or no-name products gaining traction?** One consumer health care company found that store-brand products had significantly grown unit share of the budget-conscious tier of the market over the previous five-year period. The branded health care company had grown revenue and profits over that time period, but the early warning signal precipitated a necessary focus on the store-brand threat.

3. **Are market leaders growing dollar share at the expense of unit share?** One consumer products company thought it didn't have to worry about disruption because its dollar share of the overall market had grown from 30 percent to 35 percent after it launched a new, feature-rich, high-end product. However, it achieved that growth by substantially pushing up the price of its product. The product appealed deeply to a smaller group of consumers than previous product launches, with many consumers hesitant

to upgrade. While the financial results looked good, the signs of overshooting indicated reason for concern.

4. **Is a large group of customers locked out of a market because solutions are too expensive?** If consumption is limited to wealthy customers or customers in developed countries, or, if you sell to businesses, only the largest companies, it is a sign that there is a group of potential customers who are overshot by existing solutions. In GE's case, for example, specialists and diagnosticians couldn't afford high-end ultrasound equipment.

It is worth paying careful attention to these warning signs. When overshooting sets in, companies find that growth strategies fail to deliver results and that previously easy-to-ignore attackers start gaining share at a rapid pace. Spotting overshooting requires art and judgment. Overshooting tends to start in the least-demanding tier of the market and work its way up. So look first at relatively undemanding customers. Also remember that it is very rare for a market to be overshot along *all* dimensions; overshooting happens along *particular* performance dimensions.

Signs that you have overshot a tier of the market could indicate the need to launch a defensive play against would-be attackers. Signs that a competitor in a different industry has overshot a tier of the market could create an opportunity to play offense. In either case, develop a solution that will resonate with the overshot customer.

Step 2: Develop Viable Low-cost Solutions

Winning in the low end typically requires introducing a low-cost solution (the Pampers example later in this chapter shows how sometimes you can win in the low end with a premium priced product). The first part of providing a low-cost solution involves ensuring that you cross basic perform-ance thresholds—offering good enough performance—in order to have a right to compete in a market. Consider a free, but inaudible, mobile phone, or a $200 laptop computer with five minutes of battery life. Low prices are irrelevant if a product is nowhere near good enough to get the customer's job done.

The second part of creating a low-cost solution is deter-mining how to smartly trade off performance along overshot performance dimensions to drive prices down and to invest in different performance dimensions that delight the con-sumer. Remember, it isn't simply about defeaturing or strip-ping out cost; it is about refeaturing in order to get the low-end customer's job done.

Consider the Flip Video, a camera made by Pure Digital Technologies. The product won't win any awards for the quality of images it captures. On the other hand, it is simple, easy to use, and relatively inexpensive. A camera with thirty minutes of capacity costs $100; a camera with sixty minutes costs $150. The device connects easily with a home computer, allowing fast download of video.

Think about how Pure Digital refeatured a traditional video camcorder to compete at the low end. Lower image quality and less storage capacity allows Pure Digital to charge low prices. The company crosses basic performance thresholds for these areas, however, and because the target customer is sharing video on Web sites like YouTube or via e-mail, Pure Digital's quality is certainly good enough. And Pure Digital excels on dimensions other camcorders don't consider, like the simplicity of sharing video. Connecting the device to a computer and uploading video clips takes mere minutes. The device is also very small, easily fitting into a purse or pocket.

To the target customer, Pure Digital gets the "help me quickly and easily share short video clips over the Internet" job done *better* than existing solutions. Pure Digital sold more than a million Flip Videos in 2008 to customers who were all too happy to trade off video quality for a device that is unobtrusive and affordable.

Similarly, think about how First Solar has driven disruptive growth in the photovoltaic industry. Its cadmium telluride-based solar cells are not as powerful as industry standard high-grade silicon cells, but they are significantly cheaper.

Solar scientists and research labs have long focused on increasing the efficiency with which solar cells convert sunlight to power. They have operated under the principle that generating more power from each photovoltaic cell would help make solar energy a viable alternative to conventional electricity. Consequently, the industry has almost exclusively featured high-powered electronic-grade silicon as its material of choice. However, increased demand for solar cells drove up the price of silicon to the point where lower-powered solar technologies using different base materials became more cost effective.

For many customers, cost, not physical space, is the biggest barrier inhibiting adoption of solar technologies. Would-be consumers can install more of First Solar's less-efficient panels over a larger area to generate equivalent amounts of electricity for a sharply lower cost per watt than they would have achieved with conventional silicon panels. (As of this writing, First Solar panels cost about $1.15 per watt, compared to about $3.00 or more per watt for conventional silicon solar cells and about $1 per watt for standard energy-generation from coal or gas.) First Solar's revenues exploded over the 2000s, growing from about $500,000 in 2002 to more than $1 billion in 2008.

It is critical to keep the customer, their job-to-be-done, and their view of quality at the center of discussions about performance trade-offs. For example, a global manufacturer of utility vehicles was trying to defend against a competitor that offered similar performance at sharply lower prices. As it tried to respond, development teams had fierce debates about the need to include features like electronic engine controls, a welded step, or all-weather wiring.[2]

A series of quick focus group activities and targeted surveys revealed that the company's prized electronic engine-control system really only made a difference when a customer pushed the vehicle to its limit. The rarity of this circumstance made most customers unwilling to pay extra for the feature. A traditional engine without electronic controls was good enough. So, here was an opportunity to lower prices. The company also decided to eliminate all-weather wiring, because much of the vehicle's wiring system was not exposed to the elements during routine vehicle operation and consumers didn't even know that the system used robust all-weather wire connections. On the other hand, customers perceived the bulky, strong appearance of the welded step to be a sign of quality (even though it was technically no stronger than a bent-metal design), so it was retained.

Exploring customer-derived insights feature by feature forced managers to make clear trade-offs and provided deep insights that helped the company develop a winning response strategy.

"Good Enough" Can Be Great

Good enough can be a scary phrase to many companies. Of course, in an ideal world, companies would introduce pitch-perfect products that are easy to use and affordable. The reality is that there often are trade-offs among basic performance, ease of use, and price. Most established companies implicitly favor sacrificing ease of use and price in the name of performance out of fear that sacrificing raw performance will render their products inferior in the eyes of customers (See "Cannibalization and Brand Dilution" for a discussion of other common concerns about low-end strategies).

But quality is relative. A company's view of performance rarely matches the market's view of performance. In fact, overshooting often occurs when a company mistakenly projects its own performance demands on the market. It is essential to

CANNIBALIZATION AND BRAND DILUTION

One reason established companies avoid loving the low end is they worry that the net result will replace high-margin business with low-margin business. Of course, that can happen, but low-end businesses can also grow markets. A company should worry less about how it will kill itself and think more about all the markets it can't reach. Managed correctly, disruption can be additive, not cannibalistic. Further, it is hard to stop the forces of cannibalization and commoditization. Companies should ask: if we don't do it, will someone else? Frequently the choice isn't between high margins and low margins; it is between high margins and *no* margins. Finally, if there is no disruptive competitor on the horizon, companies can think about creating a "break glass in case of emergency" plan. Once they see signs that an attacker is looming, they can take the product off the shelf. This can destroy the oxygen the competitor needs to move up market.

Another concern about loving the low end relates to brands. Managers inside established companies often worry that following a low-cost path will destroy a brand they have worked hard to build. Of course, you don't want to confuse customers by telling them a brand that meant one thing in their eyes now means something else. However, the right use of sub-brands can help to alleviate this concern. The parent brand or company name can signify that the solution is good, but the sub-brand can indicate that the product or service targets a particular problem. The right use of sub-branding (for example, Kodak FunSaver, Nintendo Wii, or Tide to Go pen) can allow companies to successfully introduce disruptive products under parent brands. Remember, disruption done correctly helps to bolster a brand by helping customers solve an important problem in their lives. In fact, a company might do more damage to its brand by needlessly overshooting and confusing its customers.

avoid overengineering products in ways that are meaningless to customers. What would happen if you intentionally lowered raw performance in the name of simplicity, convenience, accessibility, or affordability? What new markets could you serve? What new consumption could you enable?

It's Not Always About Low Prices

The success of discount companies like Wal-Mart and McDonald's in the fourth quarter of 2008 led many companies to think about how they could appeal to the growing pool of value-conscious customers. A natural inclination for most businesses is to slash features, reduce package size, and reformulate products to reach lower price points. However, loving the low end isn't just about having the lowest prices. The key is delivering products and services that the end-consumer considers to be good value.

Step back to 1961. The United States was emerging from a recession. Procter & Gamble was getting ready to commercialize disposable diapers. The diapers were expensive—seven times the price of today's diapers—so the company naturally thought wealthy parents would snatch up the product. Much to P&G's surprise, lower-income consumers embraced the diapers. It turns out the convenience factor mattered more to consumers who didn't have their own washer and dryer. Disposable diapers reduced trips to the laundromat and gave consumers—many of whom were hourly workers—the precious gift of time.

A consumer testimonial in the book *Rising Tide* sums up the benefits nicely: "P&G once received a phone call from a woman who lived in a NYC tenement building. Without Pampers, the woman said, she was forced to take a pail of soiled diapers down four floors and then walk through an unsafe neighborhood to the coin laundry located two blocks away."[3]

Loving the low end isn't just about low prices. Understanding consumers and what matters to them might highlight ways to sell products that appear expensive but are uniquely positioned to help lower-income consumers get their important, unsatisfied jobs done.

Step 3: Build a Viable Low-end Business Model

At an innovation conference a couple of years ago, an audience member asked Kal Patel, then head of strategy for retailing giant Best Buy, what the company did about its bad customers.

"There are no bad customers," Patel responded. "Only bad business models." Patel's point was that no customer group is inherently profitable or unprofitable. Seemingly unprofitable customers—who aggressively seek discounts and rapidly return merchandise—can become profitable if matched with the right business model. For example, a coupon-serving Web site like CoolSavings.com or a vibrant secondary market for would-have-been-returned products could be financially attractive ways to serve those previously undesirable customers.

A company that found success by building a business model to love the low end is fast-food king McDonald's. Interestingly, the company didn't seem to be a game changer when brothers Richard and Mac McDonald formed the business in 1940. At the time, it looked like any other hamburger restaurant, where consumers would drive in, park, and receive custom-made food.

As Eric Schlosser and Charles Wilson wrote in *Chew on This*: "By the end of the 1940s, however, the McDonald brothers had grown tired of the drive-in business. They were tired of constantly looking for new carhops and cooks as the old ones left for jobs that paid more money. They were tired of replacing the dishes, glassware, and silverware that their teenage customers often broke or stole. And they were tired of their teenage customers. The brothers thought about selling their restaurant. Instead, they decided to try something new."[4]

In 1948, the McDonald brothers fired all their carhops, closed their flagship store, installed new equipment, and reopened three months later with a novel approach for preparing food. Instead of having a single skilled cook who would custom-make orders, McDonald's simplified the menu so that less-skilled people could prepare the same thing over and over again. All McDonald's menu items could be eaten one-handed while consumers were driving. It was Henry Ford's assembly line approach applied to food service. The brothers called the model the "Speedee Service System." It made it much easier to hire and fire cooks, and allowed McDonald's to lower prices and prepare food faster. The new business model began to take off. In 1953, the company started franchising its stores to other entrepreneurs. Franchise owner Ray Kroc bought out the brothers in 1954 and scaled McDonald's into today's global powerhouse.

A business model is often the hidden inhibitor to incumbents loving the low end. Ask why Cisco Systems struggled in two separate efforts to get into the home and small business market during the 1990s. One senior leader noted, "What we learned through that entire process was that it was not a question of products, but one of business model. The high R&D, high support cost, high sales cost, which works great in an enterprise and service provider environment, is not the right one for a consumer model."[5]

To overcome the business model hurdle, Cisco purchased Linksys, whose core business was selling routers to individuals and small businesses through retail channels. Cisco made the acquisition not to get Linksys's technology, but to gain access to an appropriate business model for markets that looked much different from its core corporate market.

The general lesson here is that having the right product or service offering is a good starting point, but it's only one piece of a winning business model. As my colleague Mark

Johnson noted in a 2008 McKinsey Award–winning *Harvard Business Review* article, the other key components of a business model are the profit model and the key resources and processes that support the business.[6]

A good example of an incumbent realizing low-end growth through business-model innovation is financial services powerhouse ING. In 1997, the company launched ING Direct, a purely online banking model. Without physical bank branches, ING has very low overhead and charges low prices (which, in the retail banking world, means higher interest to consumers). The low-cost model has been a runaway success, allowing ING to reach into new markets and serve new customers.

Low-end attackers need to pay particular attention to three components of the business model. The first component is the *sales model*. Companies often instinctively try to push a low-end offering via an existing salesforce. The result is predictable: the salespeople fail to prioritize pushing simple, cheap solutions when they have more complicated, expensive ones that promise higher commissions.

SonoSite struggled with this challenge. The handheld device that began to drive disruption wasn't the company's first product. Rather, it started with more traditional ultrasound products. Then, it brought out iLook. In a 2002 interview, SonoSite CEO Kevin Goodwin described the challenges he faced in getting the salesforce to push the simple product. "I had a [sales] call . . . where I literally told the sales rep to take the iLook out of the bag and show it to the physician. He didn't do it," Goodwin said. "So I asked him again. I had to ask him three times because he would not do it. And I'm the president of the company. He wasn't being defiant, he was just nervous. It was palpable."[7]

The next component to consider is the *degree of automation or standardization*. Hitting low price points with a highly customized or personalized offering can be difficult. Automation and standardization don't necessarily mean compromising quality. For instance, many traditional media companies think the advantage they have over online players like Google is "feet on the street"—a local salesforce that can hold a customer's hand through the advertising process. Many Google customers rely on automated systems to manage their campaigns.

Many small business owners don't actually want the inefficiencies of a face-to-face sales call. Small business owners want to think about advertising after normal working hours. Along many dimensions, Google's ability to offer a do-it-yourself solution is actually better service.

Similarly, India's SKS Microfinance Pvt. Ltd. has created a vibrant business that offers very small loans to consumers and entrepreneurs who would otherwise be considered too poor to receive standard bank loans. Making the microlending model economically attractive required that SKS standardize operating procedures to enable it to dramatically increase the efficiency of handling large volumes of small customers and converting those customers into cash. The company's founder, Vikram Akula, decided to model his business on McDonald's and Starbucks. His goal was to design systems and structures to profitably handle millions of small loans. He carefully mapped out the traditional process of managing microloans, looking to cut waste. He instituted simple rules, such as setting up systematic payment schedules that required borrowers to pay in multiples of five rupees so they wouldn't use coins. Basic loan-management software on shared computers in centralized offices allowed loan officers to streamline their activities and also pointed out when SKS was developing a risky portfolio with too many loans in one area.[8]

Finally, a company needs to think carefully about what it does itself versus what it *outsources*. In 2003, Tata Group Chairman Ratan Tata announced a bold plan to build a "people's car" for Indian consumers that would cost less than $3,000. To hit its target price point, Tata chose to outsource an unprecedented 70 percent of the parts for its automobile.

Step 4: Organize Appropriately

The reason companies so frequently mangle disruptive innovation is not incompetence. Rather, it is competence. In essence, companies do precisely what they are designed to do—push quality up to charge demanding customers higher prices. Getting disruption right runs counter to the way companies are organized. Success, then, requires organizing and acting in distinct ways.

The weight of historical evidence suggests that companies that are disruptive to their core business need a great deal of organizational autonomy. An oft-cited example is the retailing industry. In the early 1960s, there were hundreds of general merchandise retailers. Most of them failed to make the transition to discount retailing, but Minneapolis-based Dayton Hudson was a notable exception. It launched a low-cost subsidiary, Target, which ultimately became the company's core business. Other industry leaders such as Hewlett-Packard and IBM have followed similar approaches to create winning disruptive businesses in inkjet printing and personal computing, respectively.[9]

Contrast Dayton Hudson's success to the struggles of F.W. Woolworth. The retailer also sensed the discount retailing opportunity, but set up a "business within a business" called Woolco with tight ties to the core. Over time, the discrete offering grew to resemble the core business so much that Woolworth folded the two businesses together in 1971 in the name of efficiency. Woolworth eventually shut down Woolco.[10] This process might be repeating itself as Wal-Mart's warehouse offering Sam's Club is increasingly outpaced by Costco, a standalone warehouse retailer.

When new ventures are internally disruptive, Vijay Govindarajan, professor of international business at the Tuck School of Business, advises against mindlessly borrowing core assets. Those assets often carry DNA that can limit degrees of freedom or take the team off their disruptive course.[11] For example, borrowing a core brand might reduce initial marketing expenditures but could force a new venture to hew too closely to the traditional standards of the parent company. A salesperson trained in the ways of the core business might rely too heavily on customers he or she knows instead of cultivating the new customers needed to make the business work.

One approach is complete organizational autonomy, but that can deny access to assets that the new company should legitimately borrow. Companies seeking to borrow at least some assets from the core business should remember these five pieces of advice:

1. **Ensure strong involvement by senior managers.** Senior manager involvement ensures that the new venture gets appropriate resources and has the freedom to attack the core business if that tactic is necessary for long-term success. In the early 2000s, Teradyne, the semiconductor test equipment market leader, created a low-cost offering based on off-the-shelf components and software. Teradyne cofounder Alex d'Arbeloff was heavily involved in that company's disruptive venture, which grew to represent a substantial portion of the company's sales.

2. **Start with a clean sheet.** Anyone who has participated in cost-reduction programs knows how hard it is to whittle down to a target. It is far easier to start from zero and build up to your target. The same is true of down-market moves: the best approach involves starting with a blank piece of paper. Use a simple test to determine which core assets can be safely borrowed by asking whether an outside entrepreneur would take the asset if offered it for free. If an entrepreneur would pass on the free asset because of resulting complexity, it is a good sign that borrowing would be a bad strategic choice.

3. **Provide substantial organizational autonomy.** Every organization has unique DNA. That DNA can subtly reshape even the most disruptive idea to look like what has been done before. Autonomy, such as the freedom to break from standard operating procedures or use different systems or processes, can allow a new venture to organize and act in ways that are appropriate for its target market.

4. **Create clear rules.** While the low-end venture needs autonomy and freedom, clear rules are needed for distinguishing customers and migrating offerings from the high-cost to the low-cost channel.

5. **Don't involve the usual suspects.** The most successful managers in the core business might be exactly the wrong managers for a down-market move. Outside perspectives can be a critical way to develop a compellingly differentiated offering. Alternatively, managers who "don't quite fit" can thrive in new environments. ING Direct CEO Arkadi Kuhlman believes that outsiders helped ING Direct realize its disruptive potential. "When you start," he said, "you bring people in for the passion and the love—you hire people that are kind of different in the industry."[12]

Disrupting the Bottom of the Pyramid

One growth opportunity that remains frustratingly out of reach for many companies is what University of Michigan

Professor and acclaimed author C. K. Prahalad calls the fortune at the bottom of the pyramid.[13] Eighty percent of the world's population and 40 percent of the world's economy (adjusting for purchasing power parity) constitute just 10 percent of revenues for S&P 500 companies.[14] Most companies based in developed economies recognize that they have to find a way to tap into these markets to hit long-term objectives.

Companies have tried various approaches to crack into these markets. Some "cream skim" or offer existing products or services to the most-demanding customers in developing markets. Others create bite-sized or stripped-down versions of existing offerings at sharply lower prices. Still others seek to tweak packaging or formulation to localize their offerings. These approaches all have merit, but are largely insufficient to realize the potential in emerging markets. The process described in this chapter can help companies more reliably develop a compelling strategy to win in these markets.

My colleague Steve Wunker provides the following advice for companies seeking to realize the potential of low-end markets:

Understand the unique demands of low-income consumers.
A stripped-down, smaller-sized offering might be adequate to help low-income consumers solve their particular problems. But it might not. Low-income consumers have unique jobs-to-be-done, meaning they might place a premium on performance dimensions that don't mean as much to consumers in developed markets. Consider low-income mobile phone consumers, who will have their handsets for a long time. The phone might be their

only status symbol. They share phones with friends and family members, use phones in public places, get jostled on the minibus, and so on. These factors mean that they might be extremely concerned about scratch resistance. They might demand particular services as well. For example, a simple service that provides weather alerts to farmers could change the game in markets where access to the Internet is still extremely limited.

Recognize the critical role of the channel. Not only does the channel help get a product or service to an end-consumer, it plays a vital role in education and purchase decisions. The dispersed nature of distribution in many developing countries presents significant challenges that require substantial investment to overcome. Global brewer SAB-Miller has created competitive advantage by taking control of distribution centers for soft drinks and beers in developing markets.

Give local organizations operational freedom. Local organizations need substantial autonomy to meet the unique needs of developing markets. Relying on corporate systems might make it very difficult for local country managers to compete effectively.

Remember the tyranny of business models. Established companies have to develop new business models to reach low-income consumers in developed countries. Consider Hindustan Unilever Limited, an Indian consumer-products company that is majority-owned by global conglomerate Unilever. In the 1990s, it created a team to identify women in rural Indian villages who could be the company's direct representatives. It used a variety of means to train and educate the targeted women, such as having actors perform skits communicating key brand messages. The women then told villagers of the importance of hand washing and shampooing. Hindustan Unilever created drop-off points where the women could pick up soap and other goods. By 2006, almost fifty thousand women in the program had increased Hindustan Lever's rural penetration in India by more than 50 percent and were generating over $100 million in revenue. The company plans to reach one hundred thousand villages in India by 2010 and replicate the model in Bangladesh.

There is a fortune at the bottom of the pyramid. Companies that follow the tenets of disruptive innovation can dramatically increase their chances of reaching that fortune.

Summary

In industry after industry, market leaders have failed in the face of a disruptive attack from below. The reasons are understandable. The potency of these attacks isn't always immediately clear. And success requires dramatic strategic and organizational shifts.

Today, companies have no excuse for being blindsided by a disruptive attack. Studying past failures highlights early warning signals suggesting that disruption is imminent. Studying entrant and incumbent successes and struggles suggests clear steps companies can take to turn the disruptive threat into an opportunity.

Specifically, companies should follow the following process to love the low end:

1. Look for signs of overshooting.

2. Embrace trade-offs to build a viable low-cost solution.

3. Encase the solution in a viable business model.

4. Organize in a way that minimizes inappropriate "borrowing" of core assets.

INCUMBENTS THAT HAVE LAUNCHED LOW-END DISRUPTIONS

Charles Schwab and online banking

Chicago Tribune and RedEye

Cisco and Linksys

Dayton Hudson and Target

Dow Corning Xiameter

GE and portable ultrasound

Hewlett-Packard and inkjet printing

ING and ING Direct

Morgan, Lewis & Bockius and Morgan Lewis Resources

Teradyne and CMOS-based sensors

Wal-Mart and SAM's Club

8

Drive Personal Reinvention

F. Scott Fitzgerald famously wrote, "The test of a first-rate intelligence is the ability to hold two opposed ideas in the mind at the same time and still retain the ability to function." Unfortunately, most managers can't pass this test. The Great Disruption will require many managers to go to "innovation school" to develop the skills to master paradox.

The word *crisis* was popular in 2008. At one point or another, pundits talked about the oil crisis, the global warming crisis, the sub-prime mortgage crisis, and, of course, the credit crisis. The hidden crisis emerging from the economic rubble of 2007–2008 is how corporate leaders have to deal with a challenge for which they are completely unprepared. A generation of corporate classical musicians who found success by following precise scores and furiously pounding keys now has to become expert at improvisation.

Existing systems, structures, and development programs that were sufficient for leaders to thrive in an era of ordered capitalism are proving to be inadequate in today's increasingly turbulent times. Most leaders just aren't ready to grapple with the paradoxes that will increasingly characterize their day-to-day lives. Hope is not lost, however. Research by development psychologists and business scholars provides practical pointers for the personal reinvention required in the Great Disruption.

Change as the New Constant

Standard & Poor's index of leading U.S. companies goes back to 1923. Research by Innosight board member and longtime McKinsey director Richard Foster found that in the 1920s (when the list contained ninety companies), when a company got on that list, it would stay on for about seventy years. That meant that people who joined an S&P company might be joining the same company their parents worked for and might expect their children to work there as well.[1]

Today, a company that enters the S&P 500 index will stay on it for about fifteen years. That means if you join a S&P 500 company today, it most likely won't be an S&P 500 company by the end of your career because it will have failed, shrunk, or been acquired. Increasingly, companies that buck the trend and last thirty or more years will do so only by mastering the kind of transformation described in this book. As Foster notes, "It's an entirely different world where the balance between continuity and change has moved to change."

The Great Depression was about working hard, mastering skills, and trying to find employment. The Great Disruption is different. It is about developing the ability to be comfortable with constant change. To expect your business or function to be obsolete in a decade's time. To be ready to transform not just your company, but yourself.

For generations, the United States had a *culture* that supported entrepreneurialism and the creation of new growth businesses. Silicon Valley was the embodiment of this culture. Today, *individuals* and the *companies* they work for have to develop this ability.

Think about the seemingly paradoxical requirements facing leaders:

- I have to focus on running operations with laserlike precision without stifling creativity.

- I exist because of my big business, but "small saplings" are critical for long-term success.

- Data drives my decisions, but I have to trust intuition and judgment when data doesn't exist or is vague.

- Attention to detail and focus on numbers has allowed me to progress in my career, but too much focus on details or numbers can crowd out innovation.

- The people I trust the most are the people who deliver short-term results and never surprise me, but innovation almost always involves some kind of surprise.

- I have to leverage my capabilities to win today's battles while walking away from many of these capabilities to win tomorrow's battles.

More than ever, corporate leaders have to meet the challenge laid down by author F. Scott Fitzgerald in 1935: "The test of a first-rate intelligence is the ability to hold two opposed ideas in the same mind at the same time, and still retain the ability to function."[2]

A Generation Unprepared

How prepared are leaders to pass Fitzgerald's test? Not very, most research suggests.[3]

Developmental psychologists have demonstrated that human capacities unfold in a series of stages.[4] Each level designates a new capacity that is inaccessible in the prior stages. For example, at one level, an individual might use rules, regulations, and the chain of command to determine what is "right." At this level, the individual would have the ability to manage his or her own activities. At an intermediate level, the individual would have a strong self identity that allows them to mediate demands from different stakeholders, allowing them to manage a group of people and tasks. At a higher level, the manager might be able to manage a group of *ideas*. In other words, the manager could simultaneously see the world from multiple perspectives and integrate those perspectives together to determine the most useful approach, given their particular circumstance. Harvard professor

Robert Kegan calls these levels of leadership development individual, autonomous, and integral, respectively.[5]

Research shows that the further a manager develops, the better his or her overall managerial ability.[6] Yet, scholars suggest that the ranks of leaders who can reach a level at which they can integrate different perspectives—a prerequisite for truly grappling with paradox—is no more than 5 percent of the total manager population.

It seems counterintuitive that achievement-oriented managers haven't naturally achieved higher development levels. Michael Putz from Cisco has studied this problem for the past decade. His perspective is that the problem isn't a lack of basic intelligence, desire, or capacity. Rather, managers haven't developed the ability to grapple with paradox because they *haven't needed to*.

Modern capitalism has been on a spectacular run since World War II. Today's leaders operate global diversified businesses on an enormous scale. The ability to handle paradox has marginal incremental utility to these challenges. Of course, many would like business to take on missions, such as a broad notion of corporate social responsibility, that may demand more complex organizational and leadership structures. However, modern capitalism has largely been able to fulfill its primary mission of creating shareholder value with leaders who lack the ability to grapple with paradox.

This mismatch helps to explain a puzzling issue for disruptive innovation advocates. Harvard Business School professor Clayton Christensen clearly laid out the pattern of disruptive innovation in academic work in the mid-1990s.

Academics and practitioners have accepted the fundamental premise of disruptive innovation. The how-to of disruptive innovation is growing increasingly clear. Yet, the number of companies that demonstrated a systematic ability to disrupt is stunningly low.

A few companies have launched a *macro* disruption that enabled a number of *micro* disruptions. For example, in the 1960s and 1970s, Sony's macro disruption was miniaturization. Sony carried that disruption to televisions, radios, and portable music players. Cisco's macro disruption is the Internet Protocol (IP). Cisco has taken its mastery of IP to data, voice, and video, creating disruptive growth in a number of markets. Google's macro disruption is the rationalization of advertising, which it is bringing to a number of different markets.

A few companies, primarily those run by a founder or a charismatic CEO, have created separate businesses that were disruptive to the core organization, such as Intel's creation of the Celeron processor in the late 1990s to respond to disruptive threats in its core microprocessor markets. A few other companies run by professional managers have created one-off disruptive success, such as GE's portable ultrasound device (discussed in the previous chapter). But the list of companies that have created the systematic ability to launch different types of disruption is amazingly short.

It's certainly not a fear of new concepts and management theories; executives seem to buy and change them as easily as a new set of clothes. But executives demonstrably favor ideas that involve ways to do what they are currently doing in a more efficient, more effective manner. Systematizing disruptive innovation is a different beast. Senior executives have to think and act in ways that run counter to everything they have done to be successful in their careers. As Putz notes, they must be multi-paradigmatic in how they structure their business model, run their firms, lead their teams, and most difficult of all, see themselves and frame their identity as leaders. Put simply, leaders who want to capture the potential of disruptive innovation need to be "consistently inconsistent" with their teams and themselves, and still hold it all together and deliver results quarter after quarter.[7]

In layperson's terms, leaders have to manage two different gut instincts at the same time, one more operational and one more entrepreneurial. Few leaders—such as Apple's Steve Jobs—do this well, and even then one side of the gut usually dominates. Leaders who can personally pass Fitzgerald's test can't crisply articulate *how*, inhibiting their ability to develop and select a successor. It is not uncommon to see one of the rare great growth leaders like longtime General Electric CEO Jack Welch turn on a hand-selected successor without the self-reflective capacity to understand their own role in the unsustainability of the growth engine they left behind.

What Do You Do?

Hypercompetitive markets with shrinking windows of competitive advantage mean that the importance of embracing paradox and systematizing disruptive innovation is going from a nicety to a necessity. Developing the capacity for paradoxical leadership is a tough challenge. Chris Argyris noted in his classic 1991 *Harvard Business Review* article, "Teaching Smart People How to Learn," that the most successful professionals are the ones who have the *most* difficulty examining assumptions and behaviors in the face of failure, even when given simple guiding tools.[8]

There's no silver bullet to address this challenge, but there are some tips to help individuals and companies develop paradoxical leaders. The first step is awareness. Experts suggest that levels of self-development should be primarily a private assessment tool, not a shared metric, with data limited to select senior managers and key human resources executives.

The next step is to develop a personalized educational program that takes advantage of a leader's self-development level. This isn't your father's HR program. Putz suggests that including psychological, philosophical, or even spiritual elements in training can help leaders improve their ability to grapple with paradox.

The good news is that there are many validated instruments to measure self-development. Further, experts who have spent substantial time using well-grounded models like Kegan's are able to quickly sniff out an individual's level of self-development. They can then design personalized training programs with off-the-shelf tools to help leaders progress. The need for customized, personalized coaching can be expensive and time consuming, but the payoff can be worth it.

One human resource executive at a famously innovative *Fortune* 500 company designed a customized program for the company's top fifty leaders based on these insights. She worked individually with leaders to determine their level of self-development. She then created customized plans to help leaders achieve higher levels of self-development. Leaders who had "framework fatigue" from going through nonstop assessments throughout their careers found great insight by going through the process. They became more aware of their strengths and limitations, and developed tactical plans to address those limitations.

Strengthening Your Innovation Muscle

Customized development programs require serious corporate commitment and personal investment. And many managers don't have to worry about paradox in the near term. They do have to improve their ability to spot seemingly hidden opportunities and act in more entrepreneurial ways. Tapping into two streams of academic research can help managers strengthen their innovation muscles.

The Innovator's DNA

Here's a simple activity. Ask ten people whether successful innovators are different from the general population. Nine of the ten respondents are likely to say that innovators are, in fact, different. Interestingly enough, for a long period of time, academic research disagreed with public perception: most large-scale research rejects the hypothesis that innovators are different, in statistically significant ways.

Jeffrey Dyer at Brigham Young University, Hal Gregersen at INSEAD, and Clayton Christensen at Harvard launched a research effort to address this puzzle. The professors conducted scores of interviews at innovative companies. They followed the interviews with large sample surveys. They tried to determine what characteristics had statistically significant impact on innovation outcomes—the successful creation of meaningful new growth businesses.[9]

The professors discovered a straightforward formula. Almost all successful innovators excel at what they call "associational thinking," which is the ability to see the connection between two seemingly unconnected ideas. An example the professors cite is Pierre Omidyar, who founded eBay. Omidyar drew on his personal experience in the collectible business, observations about the limitations of newspaper classifieds, and insights into the benefits of efficient markets from previous work experience. The need for associational thinking is consistent with a long stream of research that suggests that innovation almost always occurs at the intersection of disciplines, when people look at an idea from a new perspective.[10]

Innovators then excel at one or more ways to gather stimuli that can help them make these connections. One approach is to excel at *questioning,* or relentlessly inquiring to find insights, connections, possibilities, and directions. Some innovators are always *observing,* or intensely and intentionally watching the details of the world they explore. Of course, many innovators are constantly *experimenting,* visiting new places or trying new things. Finally, *networking* can be a way to find and test ideas through accessing a diverse network of people.

Based on this research, Dyer and Gregersen have created a simple diagnostic instrument to help innovators figure out their strengths and weaknesses. The instrument functions like a Myers-Briggs Type Indicator, using a series of relatively simple questions to tease out individual tendencies. One project team at a large company used the approach to help "unstick" a struggling team. The team was working on an innovation that had the potential to create a new category. Constant squabbling was slowing progress and leading to significant frustration. A version of Dyer and Gregersen's instrument highlighted how half of the team had tendencies that favored what the professors call *discovery* skills, where they would use some of the aforementioned techniques to innovate toward a solution. The other half of the team had a bias toward *delivery* skills related to analyzing, planning, and detail-oriented implementation. Documenting the different approaches helped the team understand differences and more productively spread tasks throughout the team.

An innovator's DNA is not fixed. Research suggests that only about 25 percent of an individual's capacity for innovation is inherited. The other 75 percent is based on experience. In other words, individuals can become better at innovation.

Dyer and Gregersen offer the following tips for people who want to improve their innovation abilities.

To become better at questioning:

- Make a regular habit of writing ten questions that impose or remove constraints (e.g., what if the price of oil were $1,000 a barrel? What if it were free?).

- Hold meetings at which you spend fifteen to twenty minutes doing nothing but ask questions (a technique known as question-storming).

To become better at observing:

- Schedule regular observation excursions to watch how certain customers use a product or service.

- Carry a diary or a notebook and frequently write down observations.

To become better at experimenting:

- Intentionally complicate your life by bumping into new information and experiences. For example, attend a conference in a different industry.

To become better at networking:

- Meet with one creative person a week for a period of five weeks.

- Have lunch with three diverse people every week.

The Right Innovation Schools

Companies are increasingly asking managers to grapple with common entrepreneurial challenges, such as dealing with ambiguity, making decisions based on intuition, experimenting to find success, using a network to solve a problem, and operating in constrained environments.

Worried about what you will do if these challenges seem unfamiliar to you? You should be. Research by University of Southern California professor Morgan McCall shows that you can reasonably predict whether a manager will succeed or fail in the face of a particular challenge by looking at their "schools of experience."[11] The schools-of-experience model suggests that people have the greatest chance of success when grappling with a problem they have previously grappled with.

Consider this analogy. Imagine you have thrived in your company's core business for fifteen years. You know how to play that game, and you play it well. Then you get the call: "Jim, I'd like you to head up our new innovation effort. It's an exciting opportunity for you. We're looking for you to really show us the way here." You immediately feel a pit in your stomach. The skills you have developed won't help you in this new assignment. In essence, after perfecting the ability to hit a baseball for fifteen years, you've been told to don skates and start playing professional ice hockey.

Leaders like Jim can be phenomenally successful. They can be phenomenally intelligent. They simply haven't attended the right schools of experience for their new assignment. Individuals in organizations rarely attend schools that prepare them for common entrepreneurial challenges. For example, many line operators are rewarded for removing or minimizing ambiguity, relying on well-grounded market research, or dispassionately making decisions based on hard numbers.

Ask yourself what sorts of problems you can anticipate encountering in the future that you have not wrestled with in the past. Look for low-risk ways to give yourself an experience that builds your ability to respond to that problem. Raise your hand for an international assignment. Find a nights-and-weekend activity that is rife with ambiguity. For example, one manager in a *Fortune* 100 company who managed a multibillion-dollar division's new business development activities created a Web-based business with a family member so that he could experience what it was like to be a true entrepreneur. Consciously put yourself into circumstances where you have to develop skills that will serve you well in future assignments.

Keeping Creative Talent Motivated

Leaders face another important challenge beyond improving their own abilities: motivating creative, innovative employees who don't land an exciting innovation project. This task doesn't have to be impossible, if companies creatively tap into their collective creativity.[12]

Companies that encounter tough times naturally become more conservative. After all, it seems hard to tolerate out-of-the-box thinking when a company faces the very real prospect of downsizing due to sliding economic fortunes. Companies place premiums on getting things done and discount long-term strategic efforts that look risky and unpredictable. As this book argues, sagging fortunes do not diminish the need for innovative thinking. Companies that play it too safe can end up in trouble down the road. Not only can more forward-thinking competitors create competitive advantage that takes years to counteract, the exodus of frustrated managers can leave a company without its most valuable assets when the economy inevitably turns healthy again.

So what can a company do to harness its creative talents given the unique needs of an economic downturn? One approach is to continue to give innovators freedom to dream up bold new ideas, but tighten the leash on near-term activities. In other words, force innovators to prove their dreams are within reach through the kind of smart, low-cost experiments described in chapter 5. Alternatively, involve creative minds in core business challenges. Can they find different ways to prune portfolios or do more with less? While exploring low-cost market research techniques or finding ways to trim benefits without alienating the staff might not sound as sexy as creating the next iPod, they require creative thinking and have a deep impact on business. Further, the more a company can improve its core operations, the more it will have funding—and patience—for innovation.

Companies that don't take these actions will see their innovation muscles atrophy during an economic downturn. Imposing discipline on the innovation process and letting creative managers use their talents to help with core challenges can keep innovators in shape for the next battle.

Summary

The Great Disruption doesn't just pose challenges for organizations; it poses severe challenges for individuals. Leaders need to improve their ability to pass Fitzgerald's test of mastering seemingly paradoxical demands. While many leaders lack the level of self-development to manage this balance, careful self-assessment and a customized development plan can help to build this skill.

Innovation practitioners need to strengthen their innovation muscles. Recent research highlights how successful innovators tend to excel at associational thinking, with tendencies toward discovery skills, such as questioning, observing, exploring, and networking. Innovators can take specific actions to improve these skills. Also, would-be innovators can consciously attend schools of experience that promise exposure to common innovation challenges.

9

What's Next for Innovation?

If history is any guide, innovation will continue to flourish no matter how frigid the environment. And today's tough times might lead to seminal changes in the world of innovation.

The economy might be sick, but innovation and entrepreneurism don't have to be. There remain ample opportunities for corporate innovators and entrepreneurs to create booming businesses that transform what exists and create what doesn't.

This book's first chapter described how history suggests "on the brink" disruptive attackers are good bets in tough climates. These attackers thrive in downturns by taking advantage of teetering giants to drive into progressively more lucrative market tiers. Disruptors that merit particular attention are those that have developed a solid starting point but are small enough to have substantial room for lucrative growth.

This book's final chapter highlights ten specific disruptors (stand-alone companies or products within companies) that could emerge as powerhouses over the next few years and points to two broad areas of disruptive opportunity. Any single development could fizzle. However, past patterns suggest paying close attention to these developments in the coming years. The book concludes with parting thoughts about the future of innovation.

Disruptive Developments to Watch

1. **Skype** (2008 revenues: $550 million; 2005–2008 growth rate: 2,116 percent). *Why it is disruptive:* simple, affordable, good enough telephone and video-conference calls.

Anyone who has experienced Skype's peer-to-peer, computer-based telephony product knows that it is a real game changer. The call quality isn't always crystal clear, but computer-to-computer calls are free. The growing ubiquity of embedded cameras makes it easy for people to conduct good enough video conferences on their computers. Free video conferencing enables new behavior patterns. One of my colleagues uses Skype when he is in Asia to create a video link between his computer and a monitor in his kitchen in America. He becomes a "virtual presence" in the house, interacting with children who happen to wander in and out of the room.

EBay purchased Skype for close to $2 billion in 2005, then had to write off half that value in 2008. Yet Skype's revenues, which come from charging people to SkypeOut and call landline phones, have quietly surged. The rise of Web-enabled smartphones will bring Skype to mobile contexts, further boosting usage—and revenues. EBay might end up selling Skype, but expect the offering to continue to transform the communications industry.

2. **Cisco TelePresence** (launched in 2006). *Why it is disruptive:* finally realizes the promise of video conferencing, making it significantly cheaper and easier for people to pick up nonverbal cues.

One of recent history's greatest teases was AT&T's videophone, which was introduced at the 1964 World's Fair. In 1969, AT&T predicted that it would sell $1 billion worth of videophones by 1980. Today, video conferencing is largely a promise unfulfilled. Poor picture quality, expensive set-up, and questionable reliability have stunted video-conferencing growth. Until recently, even the best systems couldn't deliver on the real reason a corporation would want to have a video conference: to allow meeting attendees to pick up nonverbal cues without having to deal with the hassles or expenses of flying.

That began to change when Cisco launched TelePresence in October 2006. Whereas Skype features good enough video conferencing for families and friends, TelePresence (and a competing solution by Hewlett-Packard called Halo) targets corporations that want to better manage travel budgets.

Cisco's ability to master networking allows it to intertwine TelePresence with corporate networks in a way that provides breakthrough picture quality for individual discussions or small group meetings. It allows people to pick up nonverbal cues without being in the room. A handful of companies have slashed travel budgets, but invested millions in Cisco's technology to spur collaboration. Expect this trend to accelerate in 2009 and beyond.

---

3. **EnerNOC** (2008 revenues: $106 million; 2005–2008 growth rate: 980 percent). *Why it is disruptive:* creates a new market by allowing companies to become virtual energy producers.

EnerNOC sells energy-demand management services to companies. EnerNOC's services allow it to remotely control its customers' energy use. When the electrical grid is nearing peak utilization, EnerNOC can remotely lower a company's use. For example, it might dial down an office park's electricity usage on a hot summer day when home air-conditioning use is surging. Reducing the office park's off-hour electricity usage triggers significant economic and ecological savings. That office park goes from being a pure consumer of electricity to a virtual energy producer that gives capacity back to the grid.

Without building a single new power plant, EnerNOC had close to two thousand megawatts of energy under management at the end of 2008. As corporations continue to look for ways to increase energy efficiency, EnerNOC could see a real spike in demand.

4. **Facebook** (estimated 2008 revenues: $250–$300 million).[1] *Why it is disruptive:* creates a new means of social engagement, a platform for other business models (like widgets), and the potential to create a novel and powerful business model.

Facebook has gone through the usual Internet-darling hype-cycle. The social networking company grew its user base at an astronomical rate from its founding in 2004 to 2008. An early deal with Microsoft provided a substantial revenue boost. An equity investment in 2007 valued the company at $15 billion. But then people began muttering about whether or not Facebook would be able to create a sustainable business model.

The company hasn't sat still. It has experimented with different models, such as having advertisements tied to recent purchases by members of a user's network. While this particular effort made privacy advocates wary and some users furious, Facebook should be commended for trying to find a disruptive way to monetize its massive user base. That focus, combined with the addition of seasoned senior leaders, like ex-Google Vice President Sheryl

Sandberg, gives the company a reasonable chance of finding a model that can drive hypergrowth.

5. **LinkedIn** (estimated 2008 revenues: $100 million).[2] *Why it is disruptive:* makes it simpler and easier for people to manage professional networks.

History is likely to say that the economic shock of 2008 killed many so-called Web 2.0 companies. Just as a handful of Web 1.0 companies, such as Amazon.com, Google, and eBay, thrived in the aftermath of the bursting of the dot.com bubble in 2000–2001, some recently formed Web 2.0 companies are sure to thrive. Facebook looks set to own the social networking space (with continued competition from MySpace and others, of course). LinkedIn is in an equally enviable position on the business side.

The company provides a very clear service for businesspeople who want to create and tap into networks. It already has a multi-faceted revenue model that includes advertising, charging users who want to run advanced searches to identify business prospects, and virtual headhunting. The company seems close to hitting an inflection point, and as some of its less well-off competitors fail, it should be able to expand its market lead.

6. **Amazon.com Kindle** (estimated first-year sales: 250,000 units).[3] *Why it is disruptive:* breakthrough business model focused on the job-to-be-done for the busy reader.

Amazon released its Kindle wireless reader in late 2007. Using technology from E Ink, the reader approximates the size of a hardcover book. Consumers can read books, specially formatted newspapers, blogs, and their own documents on the device. What is critical is that the Kindle unobtrusively accesses a wireless network, making it simple and easy for consumers to access content. Either consumers can go to the Amazon.com Web site on their computer and have content wirelessly sent to their Kindle, or they can access a specially formatted store on their Kindle.

Reviewers rightly noted that Kindle has some limitations. That's true, but what makes the Kindle special isn't the device; it is the business model. The model's simplicity has led Kindle users to dramatically increase their consumption of high-margin books and newspapers, making the Kindle a potential powerhouse for Amazon. The device's high price might slow sales, but the product line remains in excellent position to continue to drive growth. Being named one of Oprah Winfrey's favorite products in October 2008 didn't hurt!

---

7. **Allbaba.com** (2008 revenues [first three quarters annualized]: $400+ million). *Why it is disruptive:* allows small Asian businesses to reach much wider markets.

In 1999, Jack Ma founded a company designed to help Western companies access the Chinese market. The Web site bears some similarity to eBay's. Over the past decade, Alibaba.com has turned into the world's largest business-to-business exchange. In classic disruptive fashion, the primary users are small to midsized Asian companies that would otherwise find it difficult to find trading partners.

Alibaba.com (which is a division of the Alibaba Group) has a profitable business model, putting it in a solid position to weather a highly turbulent market environment. The company's stock dropped 70 percent in 2008, but the company still has significant growth potential.

---

8. **K^{12} Inc.** (2008 fiscal year revenues: $225 million; 2005–2008 growth rate: 165 percent). *Why it is disruptive:* comprehensive suite of offerings facilitates the growth of online learning.

In *Disrupting Class,* Clayton Christensen, Michael Horn, and Curtis Johnson made a seemingly bold prediction: by 2019, 50 percent of high school courses would be delivered online.[4] The authors weren't just sticking their fingers in the wind. They drew on historical data of adoption curves for disruptive innovations. One of the drivers for the adoption of online learning will be K^{12}. The company has a comprehensive curriculum and a proprietary delivery system to help make online learning a reality. It also has community-related features to connect parents with students and students with teachers. K^{12} sells its solution to virtual public schools like the Oregon Virtual

Academy, traditional schools that want to augment existing offerings, and directly to individuals.

Ronald Packard founded the company in 1999. Education experts developed K^{12}'s offering, and technology experts developed its delivery mechanism. As schools increasingly come under budgetary pressure and have to consider reducing teaching staff, online learning that has additional benefits, such as the ability to customize content based on individualized learning needs, will take off.

9. **QlikTech** (private company). *Why it is disruptive:* dramatically simplifies data analysis.

One of the paradoxes of the information revolution is that as we have access to limitless data, we often have less insight. The deluge of data can be overwhelming and can bury companies in never-ending analyses that obscure true insight. Enter QlikTech's QlikView offering.

The Pennsylvania-based company was founded in Sweden. Its roots trace back to its consulting work in the early 1990s. An effort to simply display multidimensional data led the company to create point-and-click software that makes it easy to visually represent and analyze data. Companies seeking to find prudent ways to manage in tough economic times are going to be hungry for easy, affordable ways to analyze data. QlikTech is in a great position to be the software vendor of choice to these companies.

The company is no flash in the pan; hundreds of companies around the globe have implemented its software.

10. **Hulu.com** (private company). *Why it is disruptive:* a simple, intuitive way to access content online; it provides a safe environment for advertisers looking to participate in online video.

The skeptics were ready to pounce when Hulu.com drew back its curtain in 2008. The joint venture between NBC Universal and News Corporation to provide high-quality video programming on the Internet was destined to be a dud, they said. After all, similar efforts by newspaper companies to unite to drive disruptive growth in the late 1990s and early 2000s collapsed under their own weight. How could industry insiders compete with Google's YouTube.com or against heralded start-ups like Joost, which was founded by the creators of Skype?

But then the skeptics started to play around with Hulu.com. They praised its clean interface and its deep library. The high-quality content has allowed the company to charge significant premiums for advertising, compared to user-generated sites like YouTube. As the company adds more content and experiments with different business models, it looks positioned to be a rare story of incumbents successfully mastering disruptive growth.

Entrepreneurs are sure to plant other disruptive seeds in the tough economic climate. The health care industry is particularly primed for disruptive innovations that make care delivery simpler and more affordable. For example, in 2009 Johnson & Johnson hopes to receive approval from the Food and Drug Administration to introduce a device called Sedasys. The device essentially disrupts anesthesiologists by allowing nurses assisting with procedures like colonoscopies to deliver anesthesia. Physicians can provide better service to patients and streamline their operations. As Clayton Christensen and coauthors noted in *The Innovator's Prescription,* there is substantial room for medical device companies to drive disruptive growth by making simpler devices that enable lesser-trained practitioners to deliver affordable care in more convenient, cost-effective locations.[5] Developments that allow increasingly precise diagnosis will further fuel disruptive change in health care.

It's also worth monitoring so-called "cleantech" companies that promise to reduce dependency on fossil fuels and create more environmentally friendly solutions. Venture capitalists and governments have significantly stepped up investment in these companies in recent years. Even as market conditions deteriorate, the focus on cleantech is likely to continue. A rising bar will make it even more important that cleantech companies follow legitimately disruptive approaches. Ener-NOC (discussed earlier) and First Solar (discussed in chapter 7) were early cleantech disruptors. A number of companies following disruptive approaches could emerge in 2009 and 2010. For example, Ottawa-based Magenn Power has created a wind turbine that floats one thousand feet above ground where steady currents help to produce consistent power. Magenn's products are easier to deploy than other wind turbines, which allows the company's products to be scaled up or down depending on a specific site's power needs. Magenn's solution could be a great way to bring power to the developing world.

Former SAP executive Shai Agassi has a similarly disruptive approach in the electrical vehicle market. While many companies in the space are targeting the Holy Grail—a low-cost battery that can go hundreds of miles between charges—Agassi's Better Place is seeking to develop a new business model that uses existing battery technology. Specifically, Agassi hopes to decouple the battery from the car, creating a model in which consumers pay a monthly subscription fee to access a network of charging sites and service centers where they can swap spent batteries for fresh ones. Instead of pulling into a gas station to refill your tank, you'll pull into a battery service station to exchange your used battery.

Analysts who want to determine which of these—or any other—disruptive developments will accelerate or decelerate should watch for two factors:

1. **A clear focus on the customer's job-to-be-done.** Disruptors always need to be sure that a laser-sharp focus on how the *customer's* definition of quality drives decisions about product performance thresholds and trade-offs. This customer-centric perspective is a best practice in any economic environment. However, in tough times

it is essential to avoid overengineering products in ways that are meaningless to customers. This customer-focused approach reduces costs and appeals to increasingly value-conscious consumers.

2. **Prioritization of profits over growth.** The tightening of capital markets reinforces the mantra of the most successful disruptors to be "patient for growth, and impatient for profits." Many disruptors design business models that enable profitability to be an option at an early stage. The push for early profits buys time to validate critical assumptions and leaves room for iteration.

Parting Thoughts

The shocks that rocked the world economy in 2008 are without recent precedent. No one knows for sure what long-term changes will result from the reverberations. Companies might feel an overwhelming desire to return to the corporate equivalent of comfort food—a focus on operating the core business as effectively as possible. Entrepreneurs might polish off their résumés and seek safe haven at a big company that appears better positioned to weather the storm.

Unfortunately, there are no safe havens in the Great Disruption. Companies that turn inward are sowing the seeds of their own destruction by creating opportunities for disruptive attackers to pull profits out of existing markets or create defensible competitive advantage in new markets. Simple survival isn't sufficient. Companies have to continue to invest in growth and innovation, or face the consequences.

Looming constraints might seem to make innovation an impossible task, but this book has shown how the silver lining for innovators is that the forced discipline of tough economic times can help innovation. Tough economic times force you to do what you should have been doing already. Excess is a root cause of many innovation struggles. Companies and entrepreneurs that have the right mind-sets and take the right actions can innovate better, faster, and cheaper.

There is a general consensus that the current economic situation is the worst since the Great Depression. Innovation didn't freeze in that period. New companies formed. Remember how the Revson brothers used money from loan sharks and creative distribution approaches to get their Revlon nail-polish business off the ground in the early 1930s. Stanford University classmates Bill Hewlett and Dave Packard famously formed the high-technology titan in a garage in 1938. Companies like General Foods, Macy's, Texas Instruments, Tyson Foods, Ethan Allen, Polaroid, and Progressive Corp. also got their starts in the 1930s. Big companies innovated as well. A scientist at chemical giant DuPont discovered neoprene, the world's first synthetic rubber, in 1930. As noted in a *McKinsey Quarterly* article, "Although the company's price levels and sales fell by roughly 10 and 15 percent, respectively, that year, DuPont boosted R&D spending to develop the new technology commercially. A buyer's market for research scientists and low raw-material prices helped the company to keep the cost of its research investments manageable."[6] Neoprene went on to be one of the major innovations of the twentieth century, with neoprene components in every automobile and aircraft manufactured in the United States by the end of the 1930s. In the face of economic distress, DuPont also invested to create one of the world's first corporate research programs, which led to the creation of other materials such as nylon.

There are reasons to expect more success stories in the Great Disruption than in the Great Depression. Over the past decade, the fog that has historically shrouded innovation has begun to dissipate as companies combine well-grounded academic research and their own field experience to markedly improve the productivity and pacing of their innovation efforts. Entrepreneurs can draw on low-cost tools to dramatically lower the cost—and risk—of starting new ventures.

The world of innovation could change substantially in the next few years. Why does the venture capital industry exist? At least one reason is the failure of large companies to innovate. Why do companies spend so much on advertising? At least one reason is the failure of large companies to come up with products and services that people actually want. Why do companies spend so much on mergers that they know will destroy value? At least one reason is the failure of large companies to create organic growth businesses with any kind of reliability.

Companies that are building processes to put well-grounded patterns of innovation to work are addressing these failures. Improvements in the innovation success rate—further fueled by the good discipline imposed by forced scarcity—will lead to unanticipated changes in the broader world of innovation.

Hope is not lost. Opportunity remains. Whether your company looks back and remembers the current economic circumstance as the beginning of the end or a kick start to transformation depends on your actions. The choice is yours.

APPENDIX

Selected Experiments
from *The Innovator's Guide to Growth*

Internal best-practice assessment. Talk to other people in the company who have addressed similar assumptions and risks to see how their efforts panned out. Use this information to assess whether you prioritized your assumptions and risks correctly. Always be careful of assuming you can be better than the best.

Secondary market research. Focused external research helps to quickly spot developments in a market space or gives a window into the actions of competitors.

External benchmarking. Look to the external market to see how other companies addressed similar issues. If your success is predicated on doing something better than it has ever been done, at least ask whether your assumption is reasonable. Market research or analyst reports are good sources for external information, as are consultants who specialize in an industry. Of course, remember that market research reports describe what has already been done, and experts are experts in what has been done before, not necessarily what could be done.

Business modeling or simulations. Combine your financial assumptions to see how the business model might work. Run scenarios to see what happens when assumptions change. Use this approach to find the real pivot points in your model. Also try to find assumptions that influence several others.

Competitive war games. Put yourself in your competitors' shoes and imagine what they would do in response to your approach. This exercise helps you understand how you can influence your strategy so it looks unattractive to your competitor. It also helps you develop systems that spot competitive moves early.

Patent analysis. Patents hold a wealth of information about an emerging market space. Patent activity or regulatory permit filings indicate how companies are approaching a space well before they announce official strategies.

Focus groups. Focus groups are useful ways to start conversations with customers. Be careful, however, about reading too much into a single focus group. One loud voice can dominate discussion, and it's always dangerous to draw conclusions from a sample size of six. Try to bring stimuli to the focus group to encourage expansive discussion.

Thought leader roundtable. Bringing together thought leaders in a defined space with a diverse set of perspectives helps you see things you might otherwise miss. Consider a way to have regular interactions with thought leaders, such as a standing advisory board.

Customer observations. Observing customers is a great way to identify the real innovation jobs that people are trying to do. While it takes time and can be expensive, sometimes there is no substitute for getting out in the field and watching a customer try to solve the problem you are hoping to help them solve or use the solution you are providing to them.

Concept tests. These tests involve describing a fully formulated concept to a customer to assess his or her willingness to purchase it. Concept tests should be used carefully for new-to-the-world or game-changing initiatives.

Quantitative market research. More detailed market research helps in developing market sizes, understanding how customers would trade off feature improvements, and identifying customer clusters. It is getting easier to design and execute good quantitative research using the Internet and other means.

Prototypes. No matter how much effort you expend, it is hard to get meaningful feedback for an idea described on paper. Similarly, there can be unpredictable interactions between components of a product that are invisible until you actually build the product. Physical or virtual prototypes can test those interactions, while also providing a more tangible vehicle to garner customer feedback. Some managers think that prototyping is only relevant for companies that make physical products. Creating Web screen shots or detailed process maps are helpful ways to develop a deeper understanding of intangible offerings. A simulated conversation between a customer and a salesperson is another way to prototype a service concept.

Test markets. Some of the most important assumptions, such as pricing, relations with the channel to market, and buyer behavior, are hard to simulate or test accurately until you actually get to market. Creating a localized test market in a particular geography, or among a particular group of customers, provides critical insight into these variables. It is important to try to simulate real market conditions. In other words, it is possible to rig the test market so it apparently succeeds, but that is not in a company's long-term best interests.

NOTES

Chapter 1

1. See http://www.djindexes.com/mdsidx/downloads/DJIA_Hist_Comp.pdf. The eight new companies on the 2008 list are AIG, AT&T (the "old" AT&T was on the 1998 list; the one on the 2008 list was actually SBC), Bank of America, Home Depot, Intel, Microsoft, Pfizer, and Verizon.

2. Roger Babson, "The Recovery from the Great Panic of 1873," *New York Times*, April 9, 1911, http://bigpicture.typepad.com/comments/2008/10/the-great-panic.html.

3. "Ka-Ching! Ka-Ching! The History of Cash Registers," Museum of American Heritage, http://www.moah.org/exhibits/archives/kaching.html.

4. David B. Sicilia, "Cash Flow," *Inc.*, June 1998. http://www.inc.com/magazine/19980615/1088.html.

5. "NCR History," Sinclair Community College, http://www.sinclair.edu/academics/lcs/departments/his/OhioHistory/NCRHistory/.

6. Museum of American Heritage.

7. Data shared with the author by Procter & Gamble Chief Technology Officer Bruce Brown.

8. Recession dates came from the National Bureau of Economic Research, http://www.nber.org/cycles.html. There were seventy-nine years between 1849 and 2008 that had at least some period of an official recession. Company founding dates were obtained from Wikipedia and additional research by the author. If company foundation were completely random, we'd expect roughly 58 percent of companies to have formed in recessionary periods (seventy-seven years between 1849 and 1983, the date of the formation of the "youngest" Dow Jones component, Verizon). So it appears recessionary times have some impact, but much smaller than we might have expected.

9. The introduction to Scott D. Anthony, Mark W. Johnson, Joseph V. Sinfield and, Elizabeth J. Altman, *The Innovator's Guide to Growth: Putting Disruptive Innovation to Work* (Boston: Harvard Business Press, 2008) describes the statistical justification of this statement.

10. See Scott D. Anthony and Tim Huse, "How Do Disruptors Perform in Recessionary Times?" December 10, 2008. http://www.innosight.com/innovation_resources/insight.html?id=693. Financial data for these calculations came from Thomson Financial and Compustat; all calculations were made by the author.

11. Clayton M. Christensen, *The Innovator's Dilemma: When New Technologies Cause Great Firms to Fail* (Boston: Harvard Business School Press, 1997).

12. One natural question is whether all small companies grew at similar rates. They didn't—in fact the 8,200 or so public companies with less than $1 billion in revenue in 1999 saw collective revenues dip by 4.2 percent a year between 2000 and 2002. Up-and-coming disruptors have outperformed the small-company sample by wide margins consistently over the past thirty years. See Anthony and Huse, "How Do Disruptors Perform in Recessionary Times?" for complete data.

13. Bronwyn Fryer and Thomas A. Stewart, "The HBR Interview: Cisco Sees the Future," *Harvard Business Review*, November 2008, 76.

14. Interview with Innosight, October 13, 2008.

15. Amy Bernstein, "Making Innovation Strategy Succeed," *Strategy+Business*, January 8, 2008, http://www.strategy-business.com/li/leadingideas/li00057.

16. Unless noted, figures represent respondents who gave scores of four or five to a question. For further findings, email santhony@innosight.com.

17. In an excellent 2008 book, Steven Spear noted that "high-velocity organizations" such as Toyota, Southwest Airlines, and Alcoa that embrace perpetual learning can create long-term advantage through operations. These organizations have indeed been excellent at driving disruptive growth and recognizing market transitions before competitors. See Steven Spear, *Chasing the Rabbit: How Market Leaders Outdistance the Competition and How Great Companies Can Catch Up and Win* (New York: McGraw-Hill, 2008).

18. See, for example Chris Zook and James Allen, *Profit from the Core* (Boston: Harvard Business School Press, 2001); and Paul B. Carroll and Chunka Mui, *Billion-Dollar Lessons: What You Can Learn From the Most*

Notes

Inexcusable Business Failures of the Past 25 Years (New York: Portfolio, 2008).

Chapter 2

1. See http://en.wikipedia.org/wiki/Coca-Cola_Vanilla.

2. Interview with Innosight, October 13, 2008.

3. Clayton M. Christensen, Stephen P. Kaufman, and Willy Shih, "Innovation Killers: How Financial Tools Destroy Your Capacity to Do New Things," *Harvard Business Review*, January 2008, 98–105.

4. Scott D. Anthony, Matthew Eyring, and Lib Gibson, "Mapping Your Innovation Strategy," *Harvard Business Review*, May 2006, 112.

5. Scott D. Anthony and Leslie Feinzaig, "Innovating During a Recession," Forbes.com, July 8, 2008. http://www.forbes.com/2008/07/08/recession-innovation-retailing_leadership_clayton_in_sa_0708claytonchristensen_inl.html.

6. See http://www.netmba.com/strategy/matrix/bcg/.

7. For specific ways to map out S curves, see Richard N. Foster, *Innovation: The Attacker's Advantage* (New York: Summit Books, 1986).

8. Clayton M. Christensen, Scott D. Anthony, and Erik A. Roth, *Seeing What's Next: Using Theories of Innovation to Predict Industry Change* (Boston: Harvard Business School Press, 2004).

9. Michael C. Mankins, David Harding, and Rolf-Magnus Weddigen, "How the Best Divest," *Harvard Business Review*, October 2008, 92–99.

10. Mankins, Harding, and Weddigen, "How the Best Divest."

11. Richard N. Foster and Sarah Kaplan, *Creative Destruction* (New York: Doubleday, 2001).

Chapter 3

1. Clayton M. Christensen, *The Innovator's Dilemma: When New Technologies Cause Great Firms to Fail* (Boston: Harvard Business School Press, 1997).

2. Scott D. Anthony, Mark W. Johnson, Joseph V. Sinfield, and Elizabeth J. Altman, *The Innovator's Guide to Growth: Putting Disruptive Innovation to Work* (Boston: Harvard Business Press, 2008).

3. Anthony, et al. *The Innovator's Guide to Growth.* Chapters 2 and 4 provide more information about these concepts.

4. Clayton M. Christensen and Michael E. Raynor, *The Innovator's Solution: Creating and Sustaining Successful Growth* (Boston: Harvard Business School Press, 2003). See specifically chapter 3.

5. Ian C. MacMillan and Larry Selden, "The Incumbent's Advantage," *Harvard Business Review*, October 2008, 111–121.

6. Innosight's "Meeting the Growth Imperative" Summit, August 7, 2008.

7. For more about the introduction of condensed soup, see http://www.madehow.com/Volume-7/Condensed-Soup.html and http://inventors.about.com/od/foodrelatedinventions/a/Campbell_Soup.htm.

8. Anthony Hallett and Diane Hallett, *Entrepreneur Magazine Encyclopedia of Entrepreneurs* (New York: John Wiley and Sons, 1997).

Chapter 4

1. Scott D. Anthony, Mark W. Johnson, Joseph V. Sinfield, and Elizabeth J. Altman, *The Innovator's Guide to Growth: Putting Disruptive Innovation to Work* (Boston: Harvard Business Press, 2008); see also Scott D. Anthony, Mark W Johnson, and Joseph V. Sinfield "Driving Growth Through Innovation," *Financial Executive*, October 2008.

2. "Nintendo Chief: Man Behind Casual Games Boom," *Reuters*, December 8, 2008.

3. Clayton M. Christensen and Michael E. Raynor, *The Innovator's Solution: Creating and Sustaining Successful Growth* (Boston: Harvard Business School Press, 2003).

4. John Jewkes, David Sawers, and Richard Stillerman, *The Sources of Invention* (New York: St. Martin's Press, 1959).

5. Amar V. Bhidé, *The Origin and Evolution of New Businesses* (Oxford, England: Oxford University Press, 2000).

6. See http://www.intel.com/capital/about.htm.

7. A. G. Lafley and Ram Charan, *The Game-Changer: How You Can Drive Revenue and Profit Growth with Innovation* (New York: Random House, 2008).

Chapter 5

1. Michael Hammer and James Champy, *Reengineering the Corporation* (New York: HarperCollins, 1993).

Notes

2. See, for example, Clayton M. Christensen and Michael Raynor, *The Innovator's Solution* (Boston: Harvard Business School Press, 2003), chapter 7; Robert A. Burgelman and Andrew S. Grove, "Let Chaos Reign, Then Rein in Chaos Repeatedly: Managing Strategic Dynamics for Corporate Longevity," *Strategic Management Journal* 28, no. 10 (2007): 965-979; Henry Mintzberg and James Waters, "Of Strategies, Deliberate and Emergent," *Strategic Management Journal* 6 (1985): 257; and Rita Gunther McGrath and Ian MacMillan, "Discovery-Driven Planning," *Harvard Business Review*, July-August 1995, 44-54.

3. For more on identifying and prioritizing assumptions, see Scott D. Anthony, Mark W. Johnson, Joseph V. Sinfield, and Elizabeth J. Altman, *The Innovator's Guide to Growth: Putting Disruptive Innovation to Work* (Boston: Harvard Business Press, 2008), chapter 7.

4. The quote was from a discussion with the author at the Front End of Innovation conference in Boston. For excerpts from the interview, see Scott D. Anthony, "The Game Changer," Forbes.com, August 28, 2008. Available at http://www.forbes.com/2008/08/28/pg-lafley-innovation-lead-clayton-in_sa_0828claytonchristensen_inl.html.

5. Scott D. Anthony and Clayton M. Christensen, "Disruption, One Step at a Time," *Forbes*, October 27, 2008 (available online at http://www.forbes.com/claytonchristensen/forbes/2008/1027/097.html).

6. Steven Spear, *Chasing the Rabbit: How Market Leaders Outdistance the Competition and How Great Companies Can Catch Up and Win* (New York: McGraw-Hill, 2008).

7. Spear, *Chasing the Rabbit*, 188.

8. Anthony, et al. *The Innovator's Guide to Growth*, chapter 7.

9. Scott D. Anthony, "Three Questions Every Innovation-Minded CEOs Should Ask," *Chief Executive*, November/December 2008 (available online at http://www.chiefexecutive.net).

Chapter 6

1. Howard M. Stevenson and Jose-Carlos Jarillo Mossi, "R&R," Case 386-019 (Boston: Harvard Business School, 1985).

2. Henry Chesbrough, *Open Innovation: The New Imperative for Creating and Profiting from Technology* (Boston: Harvard Business School Press, 2003).

3. Larry Huston and Nabil Sakkab, "Connect and Develop: Inside Procter & Gamble's New Model for Innovation," *Harvard Business Review*, March 2006, 58–66.

4. Clayton M. Christensen and Scott D. Anthony, "Do You Know What You Do Best?" *Strategy & Innovation* 1, no. 3 (2003).

5. Simona Covel, "Your Brain, My Brawn," *Wall Street Journal*, October 13, 2008.

6. To learn more about these and similar approaches, see Patricia B. Seybold, *Outside Innovation: How Your Customers Will Co-design Your Company's Future* (New York: HarperCollins, 2006); and Don Tapscott and Anthony D. Williams, *Wikinomics: How Mass Collaboration Changes Everything* (New York: Penguin Group, 2006).

7. Cornelia Dean, "If You Have a Problem, Ask Everyone," *New York Times*, July 22, 2008.

8. Raymond Flandez, "Help Wanted—and Found," *Wall Street Journal*, October 13, 2008.

9. Richard S. Tedlow, *Giants of Enterprise* (New York: Harper-Collins, 2001).

10. "Digital Filmmaking's Weak Link," *Innovators' Insights*, May 31, 2005. http://www.innosight.com/innovation_resources/insight.html?id=453.

11. Justin Ewers, "Cisco's Connections," *US News and World Report*, June 26, 2006.

Chapter 7

1. Scott D. Anthony, Mark W. Johnson, Joseph V. Sinfield, and Elizabeth J. Altman, *The Innovator's Guide to Growth* (Boston: Harvard Business School Press, 2008). Chapter 3 describes specific analyses to identify overshooting.

2. This example is discussed in more depth in Joseph V. Sinfield, "Gives, Gets, and the Good Enough." *Strategy & Innovation* 5, no. 6 (2007).

3. Davis Dyer, Frederick Dalzell, and Rowena Olegario, *Rising Tide: Lessons from 165 Years of Brand Building at Procter & Gamble* (Boston: Harvard Business School Press, 2004).

4. Eric Schlosser and Charles Wilson, *Chew on This: Everything You Don't Want to Know About Fast Food* (Boston: Houghton Mifflin Co., 2006).

5. Scott D. Anthony, "The Arm's-Length Acquisition," *Strategy & Innovation* 2, no. 1 (2004).

6. Mark W. Johnson, Clayton M. Christensen, and Henning Kagermann, "Reinventing Your Business Model," *Harvard Business Review*, December 2008, 50–59.

7. "Digital Filmmaking's Weak Link," *Innovators' Insights*, May 31, 2005. http://www.innosight.com/innovation_resources/insight.html?id=453

8. Scott D. Anthony, "No Bad Customers, Just Bad Business Models," *Innovators' Insights*, May 23, 2006. Available at http://www.innosight.com/innovation_resources/insight.html?id=254.

9. Clayton M. Christensen, *The Innovator's Dilemma* (Boston: Harvard Business School Press, 1997). See in particular chapter 5, "Give Responsibility for Disruptive Technologies to Organizations Whose Customers Need Them."

10. Christensen, *The Innovator's Dilemma*.

11. Vijay Govindarajan and Chris Trimble, *Ten Rules for Strategic Innovators: From Idea to Execution* (Boston: Harvard Business School Press, 2005).

12. Anthony et al. *The Innovator's Guide to Growth*, 206.

13. C. K. Prahalad, *The Fortune at the Bottom of the Pyramid: Eradicating Poverty Through Profits* (Upper Saddle River, NJ: Wharton School Publishing, 2006).

14. Clayton M. Christensen, Stephen Wunker, and Hari Nair, "Innovation vs. Poverty," *Forbes*, October 13, 2008.

Chapter 8

1. Richard N. Foster and Sarah Kaplan, *Creative Destruction* (New York: Doubleday, 2001).

2. F. Scott Fitzgerald, "The Crack-Up," *Esquire Magazine*, February 1936.

3. Some of the ideas in this section were discussed in more depth in "Integral Leadership: Overcoming the Paradox of Growth," an unpublished working paper by Michael Putz from Cisco Systems and Michael Raynor from Deloitte. Contact mputz@cisco.com for information about his research.

4. Jean Piaget's stage model of cognitive development, which informs the timing of subjects in school curricula, is the most widely known in developmental psychology. For example, algebra is taught in middle school or later based on Piaget's observation that abstract reasoning

emerges between the ages of eleven and thirteen. In a sense, the whole process of primary and secondary school education is based on, and is designed to support, the stage development of children as they grow into young adults.

5. Robert Kegan, *In Over Our Heads* (Cambridge, MA: Harvard University Press, 1994). Another useful model was described in David Rooke and William R. Torbert, "The Seven Transformations of Leadership," *Harvard Business Review*, April 2005, 66–76. The two highest levels of Rooke and Torbert's model were "strategists" who generate "organizational and personal transformation" and "alchemists" who generate "social transformation."

6. For example, the U.S. Army used Kegan's model in a research study of West Point cadets that showed a strong correlation between a cadet's level of self-development and their leadership effectiveness, with the most evolved cadets being rated the most effective leaders.

7. Scholars have argued that the right kind of organizational approach can help increase the roster of disruptive success stories. Christensen urged companies to set up separate organizations to commercialize disruptive ideas. That approach is indeed a proved path for one-off success, but denies organizations the critical learning required to systematize the creation of new growth businesses. Stanford's Robert Burgelman talks about how leaders have to use different lenses to evaluate different types of projects, and how keeping *discovery* projects separate from *delivery* projects can help to minimize organizational tension. Harvard's Michael Tushman and Stanford's Charles O'Reilly urge the creation of an "ambidextrous" organization designed to pursue both sustaining and disruptive efforts. Both are compelling suggestions, but it requires what Tushman and O'Reilly term the "rare but essential breed" of ambidextrous executives that "combine the attributes of rigorous cost cutters and free-thinking entrepreneurs" to build ambidextrous organizations. It seems that breed is rare to the point of nonexistence, and it requires more than "executive will to make it happen" to master ambidexterity. See Robert A. Burgelman, *Strategy Is Destiny* (New York: The Free Press, 2002); Clayton M. Christensen, *The Innovator's Dilemma* (Boston: Harvard Business School Press, 1997); and Michael L. Tushman and Charles A. O'Reilly III, "The Ambidextrous Organization," *Harvard Business Review*, April 2004, 74–81.

Notes

8. Chris Argyris, "Teaching Smart People How to Learn," *Harvard Business Review*, May–June 1991, 99–109.

9. This research will appear in a 2009 *Harvard Business Review* article and a forthcoming book.

10. John Jewkes, David Sawers, and Richard Stillerman, *The Sources of Invention* (New York: St. Martin's Press, 1959); Frans Johansson, *The Medici Effect: What Elephants and Epidemics Can Teach Us About Innovation* (Boston: Harvard Business School Press, 2006); and Thomas Kuhn, *The Structure of Scientific Revolutions* (Chicago: University of Chicago Press, 1962).

11. Morgan McCall, *High Flyers: Developing the Next Generation of Leaders* (Boston: Harvard Business School Press, 1998). See also chapter 8 of Scott D. Anthony, Mark W. Johnson, Joseph V. Sinfield, and Elizabeth J. Altman, *The Innovator's Guide to Growth* (Boston: Harvard Business Press, 2008).

12. Scott D. Anthony, "The Challenge of Challenging Creatives," *Talent Management*, December 2008. http://www.talentmgt.com/newsletters/talent_management_perspectives/2008/December/817/index.php.

Chapter 9

1. Dan Frommer, "Zuckerberg: Facebook Revenue Growth 'Really Strong', Still Hiring," *Silicon Alley Insider*, January 12, 2009. http://www.alleyinsider.com/2009/1/zuckerberg-facebook-revenue.

2. Brad Stone, "At Social Site, Only the Businesslike Need Apply," *New York Times*, June 18, 2008. http://www.nytimes.com/2008/06/18/technology/18linkedin.html.

3. Zach Pontz, "A year later, Amazon's Kindle finds a niche," CNN.com, December 4, 2008. http://www.cnn.com/2008/TECH/12/03/kindle.electronic.reader/index.html.

4. Clayton M. Christensen, Curtis W. Johnson, and Michael B. Horn, *Disrupting Class: How Disruptive Innovation Will Change the Way the World Learns* (New York: McGraw-Hill, 2008).

5. Clayton M. Christensen, Jason Hwang, and Jerome Grossman, *The Innovator's Prescription* (New York: McGraw-Hill, 2009).

6. Tom Nicholas, "Innovation lessons from the 1930s," *McKinsey Quarterly*, December 2008. Available at http://www.mckinseyquarterly.com/Strategy/Innovation/Innovation_lessons_from_the_1930s_2266.

INDEX

ABOUT THE AUTHOR

SCOTT D. ANTHONY is the president of Innosight, an innovation consulting and investing company with offices in Massachusetts, Maryland, Singapore, and India. He has consulted to *Fortune* 500 and start-up companies in a wide range of industries. In 2005–2006 he spearheaded a year-long project to help the newspaper industry grapple with industry transformation (Newspaper Next).

Anthony coauthored (with Harvard professor and Innosight cofounder Clayton Christensen) *Seeing What's Next: Using the Theories of Innovation to Predict Industry Change* (Harvard Business School Press, 2004) and *The Innovator's Guide to Growth: Putting Disruptive Innovation to Work*. He has authored articles in publications such as the *Wall Street Journal*, *Forbes*, *Harvard Business Review*, *BusinessWeek*, *Chief Executive*, *Sloan Management Review*, *Advertising Age*, and *PressTime* and serves as a regular columnist at Harvard Business Online.

Prior to joining Innosight, Anthony worked with Christensen at Harvard Business School, leading a group that worked to further Christensen's research on innovation. He has worked as a consultant for McKinsey & Co., a strategic planner for Aspen Technology, and a product manager for WorldSpace Corporation.

He received a BA in economics, summa cum laude, from Dartmouth College and an MBA with high distinction from Harvard Business School, where he was a Baker Scholar. He lives in Chestnut Hill, Massachusetts, with his wife Joanne, son Charlie, and daughter Holly.